OBSERVING
WHAT IS NOT
HAPPENING

OBSERVING
WHAT IS NOT
HAPPENING

Second Autobiography

Nndy Nenty

authorHOUSE®

AuthorHouse™ LLC
1663 Liberty Drive
Bloomington, IN 47403
www.authorhouse.com
Phone: 1-800-839-8640

Published by AuthorHouse   03/06/2014

ISBN: 978-1-4918-4605-6 (sc)
ISBN: 978-1-4918-4607-0 (e)

Library of Congress Control Number: 2013923322

Any people depicted in stock imagery provided by Thinkstock are models,
and such images are being used for illustrative purposes only.
Certain stock imagery © Thinkstock.

This book is printed on acid-free paper.

Because of the dynamic nature of the Internet, any web addresses or links contained in
this book may have changed since publication and may no longer be valid. The views
expressed in this work are solely those of the author and do not necessarily reflect the
views of the publisher, and the publisher hereby disclaims any responsibility for them.

Introduction

Observing What Is Not Happening is a continuation of the author's first memoir, *Where Your Knowledge Ends Is Where Mine Begins*. Six chapters of this second memoir are ageless; they stem from the Word of God. They are predicated on the Word of God.

"Observing what isn't happening" is a remark first made by Rush Limbaugh. And it was elected to be the title of my second memoir because through the wisdom, knowledge, and understanding from the Holy Spirit, I know all the ways of Man. The ways of Man are an open book to me. Man's behavior, actions, and attitudes are so obviously pronounced to me. Observing what is not happening is predicting what Man will do regardless of how long he tarries; Man will eventually do what I predict.

I'm writing this book at age thirty three, the same age Jesus Christ was before He departed the world.

The main characters in this memoir are God Almighty, Jesus Christ, and the Holy Spirit. Archangel Lucifer, Apostle Excel, Rush Limbaugh and Iifi are other prominent characters.

Everything I say in this memoir stems from the Word of God.

Book Author

Nndy Nenty is an upstage charismatic figure, a New Yorker of Nigerian descent, an author of three previous books, and a student of the Limbaugh Institute for Advanced Conservative Studies. Nndy is a servant of God, the last vestige of truth, and the forerunner of the Second Coming. Nndy is blessed with an invincible wisdom. At the age of thirty-three, Nndy Nenty was baptized.

Book Dedication

Nndy Nenty dedicates this book to
the Almighty God in Heaven.

Table of Contents

YOU READ THIS BOOK
AT YOUR OWN PERIL

Chapter 1

Sin

———∿∽⌒⌒⌒∿———

Sin

Sin originated from Heaven when Archangel Lucifer attempted to build his throne above the throne of God. When God created the Heavens, God also created the angels. Archangel Lucifer was made perfect in beauty and he was made full of wisdom. But the very moment iniquity was found in Lucifer, Lucifer was put out of grace. He was cast down from Heaven and his countenance changed. Ezekiel 28:15 states, "Thou wast perfect in thy ways from the day that thou wast created, till iniquity was found in thee." What Happens When Thunder Strikes Lightening? Christ affirmed that He beheld Satan falling like lightening from Heaven. Like lightening to earth Lucifer fell from Heaven. How the great son of the morning, Archangel Lucifer, fell from grace to grass. Angel Lucifer was his name before iniquity was found in him; and when he was cast down from Heaven, he assumed the name "Satan, the Devil." Lucifer was pregnant with iniquity and when he fell from Heaven, he conceived iniquity on earth; thus, Adam and Eve were contaminated; thus, Cain killed Abel; and a trillion more "thuses," including the gruesome murders of this generation. For that reason, the Virgin Mary was pregnant with salvation to counter the iniquity found in Lucifer. God said in Isaiah 45:7, "I form the light, and create darkness: I make peace, and create evil: I the Lord do all these things." Evil emulated from the darkness that God created. But before Lucifer was dispensed with, evil was void and concealed. That evil manifested itself through Lucifer.

Satan is the accuser of the brethren and the avenger of blood. The servant of Satan happened to be the son of perdition, Judas Iscariot. The servant of Satan is also the Antichrist, who is being readied and poised to rear his ugly head. The Prince of Persia is also the servant of Satan.

Man's actions and utterance comes with sin. Just about every deed of Man is sinful before God Almighty because sin is inherent in Man. Save for the Virgin's Mary's first child, every human being born from the womb of a woman are all sinners. Man has become a proxy for Satan. And when he assumes room temperature, Satan will be standing over his carcass. Thus he becomes the property of the Second Death, where there will be gnashing of teeth.

And when Jesus Christ came as the new Adam, Christ came to show Man the way it ought to be; the way Adam was supposed to live; the way Man was supposed to live in God's perfect will. God's permissive will was enforced because sin corrupted Adam and Eve.

What is sin? Sin is racism, hatred, bigotry, and prejudice. Sin is jealousy and envy. The whole nine yards are all definitions of sin. Prejudice and discrimination are permanent albatrosses on Man's neck. Man is embedded with sin and innately sinful. Man is married to sin and sin only divorces from Man when Man dies.

Certain anger that we exhibit is not sin. The emergence of anger from left field is not sin because it is obviously not borne out of hatred, jealously, or envy, so it is not sin. Such anger out of left field doesn't begin as sin; it only gradually morphs and becomes sin. The Bible warns, "Be ye angry, and sin not: let not the sun go down upon your wrath." The anger the Word of God was referring to was uncorrupted anger. But anger borne out of hatred, jealously, or envy is corrupted anger. Hence, such anger is sin in itself. Why was God angry and furious with the children of Israel throughout the most part of the Old Testament? There was no end in sight to God's indignation toward the children of Israel and Judah. God was angry at the children of Israel because God's anger was for the correction of Man's sins. So God's anger was not anger in itself.

Satan is sin; he begot sin. So to enjoy the pleasure of sin is to enjoy the pleasure and the savor of the Devil. Sin reigned over earth. You wholeheartedly believe that there is a God in Heaven but you love the pleasure of sin. You can't serve God on one hand and serve mammon on the other hand. You can't have your cake and eat it too. You are on the knife's edge of knowing you would be condemned to hell if you don't repent. Yet you allow the amusement and the pleasures of sin to overtake you. You love the pleasures of fornication, covetousness, idolatry, etc., more than the pleasures of eternal life.

Sin is inherent in Man but don't let your sin overtake, engulf, and control you. The journey is to make it to Heaven; the race is not for the swift but it is for those that endure. Don't let your sin surpass the Spirit of God in you.

The more righteous you are the more you recognize sin. The more pure wisdom you possess, the more you can instantly recognize a sin. And I disclose to people that I am the most sinful person on earth because I can perceive and recognize sin as clear as day. If committing idolatry, adultery, theft, and other grave and abominable sins sums up your life on earth, then there will be wailing and gnashing of teeth.

Endeavor not to sin in the presence of Man; don't sin in the presence of sin himself. Let there be no witness to your sin, save for God Himself. It's only God that witnesses my sin. I won't sin and have Man witness my sin. So I won't curse at Man, thereby making Man a witness to my sin. I would not be caught dead uttering expletive and epithets, because every idle word will be accounted for. Let God be the only witness of your sin. Any time people do or utter something sinful before me or in my presence I immediately pray to God to forgive me. It is detestable to me to witness people sin around me.

What is worse than death? It's an oversight or naiveté to believe that death is the worst event in life. And Man cries and laments till the cows come home when he loses a loved one.

Hell Fire, which is also the Second Death, is worse than death. Because of the wages of sin, all human beings born into this life on earth must die; ashes to ashes and dust to dust. It's all academic to wish death upon a fellow Man because every Man has been appointed to die—just as they were appointed to be born.

Satan is the accuser of the brethren. You put words in Satan's mouth when you sin against God. Satan condemns you when he reports you to God. Be quick to confess your sins before God with immediate effect because Satan, the accuser of the brethren, lurks around to incriminate you before God. If you are on the verge of stealing, if you are bound to covet, or if you are on the verge of committing adultery, etc.—the Devil is already standing by, lurking and waiting. He is waiting to hold you accountable to God, and at the same time he draws you closer to the sinful act—enticing and urging you to do the act while also distracting you from listening to the still small voice that advised you to refrain from what you are about to do. You don't want to lie, fornicate, and steal. You don't want Satan to go before God and recount to God: "I didn't know that Jesus Christ died and made your servant Peter a liar?" And you will put God in a difficult situation defending you. Satan will surely continue: "God Almighty, do You still intend to elevate your servant to a new position in life? Or may I rephrase my question: Do You still desire to elevate your lying servant Peter to a better position in life? A servant, that for all intents and purposes, threw Christ's sacrifice for Man under the bus. How do You, God Almighty, justify the actions of your servant?" God forbid, it was Judas Iscariot that died and made you a thief, not Jesus Christ. By and large your sin will judge you. The Devil, on the left hand side, will judge you before God, while Jesus, on the right hand side of God, intercedes for your sins before God daily.

It's incumbent for me to run away from sins and the wrongs of life every day of my life.

"You can run but you can't hide." The Word of God has already testified against all the sins of Man. So sin is perpetually waiting on the horizon to testify against you in order to justify the Word of God. And Man will be used as an instrument for sin to be manifested.

Did the sins of earth hinder Jesus Christ? Jesus could not see the end of time; it wasn't revealed to Him because He was here on earth. Earth is engulfed in sin; so since Jesus lived in a sinful place, Jesus couldn't tell the end of the world. Satan doesn't know the end of the world; Satan chomps at the bit to know when the world will come to an end. Satan eavesdropped when Christ's disciples questioned Christ about when the end of the world would be. But God Almighty did not reveal it to Jesus because Jesus was on earth. Hence, Satan is only left to garnish more souls with him to Hell Fire since he was concealed from knowing when the world will come to an end.

As the days of my life go by, there are fewer arrows in Satan's quiver against me because the material things of the world are behind me. A thousand and one material things that the world does, I resigned and divorced myself from doing, so Satan is by and large limited and grasping at straws in his attempts on me. Satan can't tempt me unless I give myself to be tempted. I see well in advance any temptation coming from the Devil. And it's left for me to either purposely fall into the temptation or rebuke it outright.

The works of Lucifer's are the works of iniquity. Destroy the works of Lucifer in your heart. Destroy the works of iniquity in your life so that you wouldn't be in danger of the Lake of Fire. When will Lucifer's legendry and legacy ends? Sin has multiplied over the years; the longer human beings remain on earth the more sin is multiplied. The spirit of racism, bigotry, and prejudice is prevalent, to say the least. It's not only beggars and panhandlers that beg; opportunities in the form of fornication, murder, and theft are on their knees begging. So the ball is in your court to let opportunity go begging; let the pleasure of sin go begging.

Being alive is sinning, and that is the whole bottom line; sinning is being alive. We should only sin because we were conceived in sin and not because we love the gratification and the pleasure of sin; we are inherent in sin. Did the sin of earth supersede the holiness of Jesus Christ when He was on earth? The sins of earth reached a summit, that even the Son of God, as holy as He was, couldn't discern the end of time. Man should only sin because every Man born into this world was conceived in sin. So it's inevitable that Man must sin. But Man should not sin with the intention and with a conscious mind.

Earthly Spirits

The seven spirits of Man are the spirit of idolatry, the spirit of blasphemy, the spirit of murder, the spirit of adultery, the spirit of theft, the spirit of deception, and the spirit of covetousness. The seven spirits of Man stem from the Ten Commandments in Exodus 20:1-17 and Deuteronomy 5:4-21. These seven spirits of Man go hand in hand.

What is opportunity? Opportunity comes in many forms; it could be adultery, theft, covetousness, etc. Opportunity is always lurking on the horizon. Don't suffer opportunity to make you a thief, a cheat, or a deceiver. Opportunity goes to and fro and back and forth. But what is opportunity? When should you suffer opportunity to go begging? If opportunity comes out of left field then suffer it to go begging because it's sudden. But if opportunity falls in your lap, don't let it go begging, because you have the time to think about what lies in front of you.

The genesis of all the spirits that ever existed is the spirit of pride. The spirit of pride came before the spirit of disobedience that corrupted Adam and Eve. God knew the thoughts of Lucifer and it was recorded in Isaiah 14:13, "For thou hast said in thine heart, I will ascend into heaven; I will exalt my throne above the stars of God: I will sit also upon the mount of the congregation, in the sides of the north." Lucifer's pride went before his fall. God drove King Nebuchadnezzar of Babylon into the wilderness after pride engulfed him. Nebuchadnezzar repented from his pride, then God rendered him back his kingship.

Daniel 4:29 says:

"At the end of twelve months he (Nebuchadnezzar) walked in the palace of the kingdom of Babylon. The king spake, and said, "Is not this great Babylon, that I have built for the house of the kingdom by the might of my power, and for the honour of my majesty?"

While the word was in the king's mouth, there fell a voice from heaven, saying, "O king Nebuchadnezzar, to thee it is spoken; the kingdom is departed from thee. And they shall drive thee from men, and thy dwelling shall be with the beasts of the field: they shall make thee to eat grass as oxen." God Almighty spared Nebuchadnezzar and punished Lucifer.

The spirit of death could be summoned by Satan. Hebrews 2:14 states that Satan has the power to take life, but without God's permission, one's life can't be taken. God is the final arbitrator. The Spirit of death dwells on earth.

The spirit of death was sent by Heaven to take the life of my younger brother. On its way, Satan met the spirit of death halfway to corrupt and deceive the spirit of death, swearing that I was the one whose life was required by Heaven. Therefore, the spirit of death came to take my last breath away, but the Son of the Highest rebuked the spirit of death, hence not permitting it to take my life. The spirit of death then returned to the sender and was instructed of who was meant to die in my family. Hence, the spirit of death returned and took my younger brother's life. Satan recognized the anointing that God had given me, so he fought tooth and nail to make certain that I was the one whose life was required of. The spirit of death was deceived by Satan that my brother, who was two years younger than I was, and who was also bigger in stature than I was, was the one to be spared.

Satan instructed the spirit of death to take the life of the one (Nndy) who was the smallest of the four children my parents had. Nsemeke saw God's face; hence, he died. Nsemeke, my brother, died even while my grandfather was still alive. Hence my brother slept with his great-grandfather.

Once upon a time, God breathed His Spirit into Man and Man became a living being. But due to Adam's disobedience, the breath that Man breathes became contaminated and befouled with sin. Man breathes out the Spirit of God and breathes in the contaminated spirits of sin.

God has given me the ability to perceive diabolical spirits in people. I can't be jealous and envious of Man because I don't aim to be like any Man in this world. God has deprived me of the spirit of jealousy, hatred, and envy.

The spirit of murder was the first spirit to manifest after the fall of Man. This happened when Cain slayed Abel. It's below my pay grade to discuss murders, homicide, manslaughter, etc. I'm not going to comment on a mass murder that befell on the month of May, and come tomorrow remark on another mass murder that befell on the month of June. There is nothing Man does that amazes me in this life. Cold-blooded killing, double-nine-style execution, and gruesome killings, etc. is unfortunately part of life on earth. Hence, the only murder that I am invested in is Cain and Abel. That is the root to all murdering. That is the only murder that I observed and recognized. Once you biblically know why it befell, then you could solve the puzzle and connect the dots. Other brutal, inhumane killings that go on in the world even in this generation are nonchalant to me; my sympathy and empathy are felt for such grave wickedness, but to me it is part and parcel of life on earth; it is part of mankind. The spirit of murder schemed and perpetuated by Cain is in every human being that is born; it just has to be provoked and then triggered. The genie will one day get out of the bottle—especially Satan roaming to and fro, looking for a loose cannon. There is no end in sight to Man's wicked and evil ways, because Cain has already gotten the ball rolling.

Joseph was a faithful servant to Potiphar; Potiphar was a captain in Egypt. Opportunity came in three forms to tempt Joseph: the lust of the eyes, sin itself, and Potiphar's wife. Opportunity presented itself before Joseph; opportunity was on his knees persistently begging for Joseph to fornicate, but Joseph refused and hence was pilloried and cast into prison. Potiphar's wife had the looks of Medusa but Joseph didn't suffer opportunity the chance to brand him a fornicator. So opportunity (sin) was astonished that Joseph let the pressure of fornication go begging, hence sin punished Joseph by incarceration.

Your hands are clean if you profoundly and sincerely warned your offspring about sex. But if you take a lenient stance and you zealously pampered your offspring, and as a result, your offspring chose a promiscuous lifestyle and went the way of the harlot, all the blame lies at your feet. You will be held accountable.

King David died and made Man a coveter, an adulterer, and a murderer. And it came to pass that David committed adultery with one of his servant's wife, and then he ordered his servant to the forefront of an ongoing war to eventually be slain. David first committed the sin of covetousness. He coveted his servant's wife and then proceeded to commit the sin of adultery by sleeping with his servant's wife. David then aided and abetted in the murder of his servant. The long and the short of David's deeds was that the opportunity to rest at his palace while all of Israel went to war made King David a coveter, an adulterer, and a murderer.

Opportunity doesn't only make a thief. Because of the spirits of sin, David couldn't overcome the opportunities that stared at his face in the form of covetousness, adultery, and murder.

If you don't sandwich a time for God from the rising of the sun until the going down of the same, then you are not living life. You are under an illusion if you think you are living life. You are learning your alphabet on how to make it to Hell Fire.

Asking for forgiveness after blaspheming against the Holy Spirit is like looking for the silver lining in a sinking Titanic. If you blaspheme against the Holy Spirit and you petition for God's forgiveness, then you have called Jesus Christ a liar. Jesus has already said a blasphemy against the Father and the Son is forgivable but a blasphemy against the Holy Spirit is unforgivable.

Lying is in certain words that come out of the mouth of Man. "If a tree falls in a forest and no Man is around to hear it, does it make a sound?" How can you prove a lie? If a Man lies to a congregation and there are no witnessed to testify against his lie, then did he tell a lie?

God Almighty directed Samuel the prophet to prevaricate the people if they questioned why he came to anoint David as King of Israel since King Saul was still the sitting king. But the lie was a commonsense lie and it had some truth in it. If you have to lie, let there be some truth to the lie. Let the lie which you narrate kill more than one bird with one stone. Let it be distinguished from a blatant lie. By and large, let the lie be sincere and let it come with the truth. It's common sense to lie if the lie is a matter of life and death or a matter of freedom. A commonsense lie could be justified.

Tell the truth to God all the time. "Thou shalt not bear false witness" is one of God's commandments, but Abraham misrepresented when asked about Sarah his wife, Jacob lied about being Esau (his older brother), and Jeremiah lied because he feared being killed. All these men were great servants of God. Jeremiah's falsification was common sense and he confessed to God first. It was a matter of life and death on Jeremiah's part, so it was a commonsense lie to save his life. A lie is not a lie when you first and foremost confess to God Almighty; therefore, what you tell Man is not a lie before God.

As long as your sin doesn't affect another human being then those sins can't judge you; your conscience can't stand against you. A judgeless sin is a sin that doesn't involve Man; it's a sin in which only God is your witness. A lie is only a lie when it affects other people. A lie is only a lie if what precedes the lie was a sin—for example, stealing something and then denying that you stole it. A lie to man is not a lie to God if you first brought the issue to God Almighty, if you first sincerely confessed to God. You can't lie to God because He knows everything. Hence, if you are untruthful to Man you are untruthful to sin. If you lie to Man without first acknowledging God, then you are a liar, a fabricator, and even a prevaricator. The rope of liars is short, so give them enough rope to hang themselves.

The commandment of God states, "Thou shall not steal." The Gospel of John described Judas Iscariot as a thief. Of the twelve disciples of Christ, Judah Iscariot was the one in charge of the money bag. Let opportunity go begging; don't suffer opportunity to make a thief out of you. Opportunity rears its ugly head mostly when no one is around; opportunity will keep begging and salivating for you to steal. Integrity is doing the right thing when no one is around.

If I should steal, if I should subject myself to theft, it implies that the spirit of theft is greater than the Spirit of God in me. God forbid. God has made me loathe the material world. So my eyes are satisfied with earthly and secular things. Hence, I look not at my neighbors to covet. The spirit of theft will be grasping at straws if it had to be greater than the Spirit of God in me.

If you accused me of theft you have to accuse me of murdering too. You can't start your accusation with theft and end your accusation with theft. You have to go all the way. I want to hear the end of it. You can't start without finishing. All this must transpire before I accept that I'm a thief. If you sin in one then you have sinned in all; if you accuse me of theft then you might as well accuse me of murder, because I'm all about the extreme. If you slap me on one cheek, you must slap me on the other cheek. You can't start without finishing. If you accuse me of theft and I try to defend myself then I stand guilty even if I didn't steal. But if you accuse me of theft and I don't retort, then you have not accused me of stealing, rather you have accused the Almighty God of theft. So only God can pardon you, I can't pardon you. Forgiving Man is out of my hands; I deprived myself from forgiving Man because God is my Potter.

Christ didn't die and make me a thief like Judas Iscariot, a murderer like Cain, a coveter, and an adulterer like David; but Christ died and made me a faithful servant of the Holy Spirit.

It's good to let opportunity go begging in most instances. I'm heedless to the spirits of sin; hence, the Spirit of God in me is greater than the spirit of lying, theft, adultery, etc. that hover around me. If you diligently heed the Word of God, then He (the Spirit of Truth) that is in you is greater than he (the spirit of sin) that is in the world. Opportunity is always hovering, looming large and poised to lure its next victim. Except in the household of Judas Iscariot, never mention rope in the house of a Man who was hanged. I perceive evil spirits in people every now and then in public places and I pray hard to the Lord. Beware of the sins that deal with Man. Murder, rape, kidnapping, and theft can't happen without involving another entity. You can lie without affecting another party but you can't steal, murder, or rape without affecting a second party. Take your last breath of fornication, thieving, and deceit, etc.

Forgiveness

If you beseeched a Man to forgive you that means you are bidding sin to forgive you. And it begs the question, how can sin forgive sin? And if Satan is the originator of sin, how can Satan who begot sin forgive sin? Is it only the Lord God Almighty who can exonerate us of our sin? You could of course ask someone to forgive you for the wrong you did, but could not specifically bid someone to forgive you of your "sins," unless Jesus died and ordained a sinner in charge of pardoning sins.

If I have to entitle myself to forgive someone for what he or she did to me, then it wouldn't be from the heart. I don't entitle myself to forgive people; it is up to God to forgive.

I have to forgive myself first before I dialogue with a loved one who has gravely offended me. And forgiving myself could take a few seconds or till the cows comes home. What should happen in the case of exonerating someone's action when the situation is ambiguous?

How can you forgive someone when the one that was unjust to you does not even acknowledge his or her action against you? Or he or she doesn't even consider that what he or she did was reprehensible in the first place? Such is the hardest of all forgiveness. If I had to apologize to Man and I knew with certainty that I was right but was being judged to be wrong, then I would apologize quoting the Word of God.

We have all sinned and fallen short of the glory of God. I won't hide in the midst of "we" so I rephrase my statement, "I have sinned and fallen short of the glory of God." And I won't utter this in passing or in lip service; I won't speak in a crusade or platitude way. I would say it from my heart.

It's impossible for Man to go a day without transgressing before God. Man is innately sinful. Man's iniquities are ever before him. I adopted Job's attitude of confessing my sins and my missing rib's sins before God. That is the confession of forthcoming sins before God Almighty.

Man's sins know no bound because Man depends on seventy times seven. Man disregards the fear of God because he is aware that God's grace will abound. Man sins because God's mercy endures forever; Man sins because Jesus Christ intercedes for him on a daily basis. But doesn't the mercy of God come with stipulation? Seventy times seven times we should forgive those who upset us so that the good Lord will also forgive us. Ask for God's mercy seventy times seven times in a day because sin is inborn in Man.

It goes without saying that Man should pray for God's forgiveness each and every passing day. Human beings and sin are inseparable. They co-exist together. So we should unequivocally seek God's forgiveness every opportunity that we have. So long as we live this mortal life, we have sinned. We have to beseech God to forgive us in every prayer we utter to God hourly or daily, because Man is inherently sinful. Just living this life is a sin in the eyes of God.

Because of the pure holiness of God, just about everything Man does or says is sinful before God; so long as Man knows the difference between good and evil. Man should live his life everyday assuming that everything he does and every word he utters is a sin before God.

If you commit a grave sin, it's because you refuse to harken to the still small voice. Like Eve, you chose the second thought of Man rather than the first thought of Man. The damage has already been done and you have supplicated for forgiveness and forgiveness has been granted. But the scare is there, the damage is done. So you have to walk a tightrope for the rest of your life trying not to suffer God to remember your past iniquities; trying to prove to God that you have really repented from that act.

Man's action and utterances comes with sin. All the sins of Man will be forgiven by the Almighty except the sin of blasphemy against God the Holy Spirit. I bid God to give me the heart to only sin ignorantly against Him rather than sinning intentionally. Those vicious men that killed Christ and those untold number of barbarous Jews and Pharisees that aided and abetted Christ's death thought they knew what they were doing. They thought they were crucifying the Man that professed to be the Son of God. But with the mercies of God, Christ, while in the throes of dying for the sins of Man uttered, "Father, forgive them for they do not know what they do."

Chapter 2

Ideology and Faith

Conservatism

I'm a no-nonsense, passionate, and an unadulterated conservative. You can't fathom the wisdom of conservatism until you become one. God has equipped me with the knowledge of conservatism. As a through and through conservative, I will always leap to the defense of conservatives.

I have reached the deepest depth of conservatism. Thanks to God for revealing Rush Limbaugh to me; I'm Mr. Conservative; I'm the quintessential image of conservatism. I know everything—lock, stock, and barrel—about conservatism. I have reached the deepest depth of conservatism and I assure you that conservatism is ecstasy, joyful, and blessed—but it doesn't guarantee salvation. I have seen the end of conservatism. After seven years as a full-fledged, unadulterated, no-nonsense conservative, I'm writing this book standing at the end of conservatism looking back to the year 2013—just as the Spirit of God took the Apostle John to see the end of the world enabled John to write the book of Revelation. I'm grateful to Rush Limbaugh and the Limbaugh institution for advancing conservative studies.

My mind is conservative and my heart is Christian. Liberalism or any other ideology that Mankind has conceived has no part in me. I'm a conservative servant; I'm proud to be a Limbaugh conservative. And certain people hope that one day I will convert and become a liberal, which won't happen unless Christ is coming again to die for us. In the first place, it's a scarlet letter to be a liberal.

I'm an unrepentant conservative. People maintain that I have been brainwashed by Rush Limbaugh and I retort that I'm to the right of Rush Limbaugh. In some instances, those with whom Rush Limbaugh would cut some slack and who Rush Limbaugh would take prisoners, I wouldn't even consider. I will grudgingly accept conservative converts but I wouldn't welcome them to conservatism. The people who label themselves conservatives would not pass the threshold of being conservative in my books.

Conservatism is hated worldwide, but not because of its substance; rather, because conservatism stands for the truth. I would rather be called a conservative than to be called a Christian. I live on being hated; I thrived on being hated. Conservatism has it flaws, albeit it was adapted in large part from the Holy Scriptures. Conservatism has no substitute; it is in a league of its own. Only the Gospel can condemn and render useless conservatism. So conservatism is the cutting edge ideology on earth. Conservatism is common sense rooted in the Word of God. Conservatism is the epitome of common sense. Conservative is all about substance.

True conservatives don't detour from conservative orthodoxy; rather, they focus steadfastly on conservatism destinations. What are conservatism destinations? Pursuit of happiness, liberty, freedom with judgment, preserving of family values and traditions, and obeisance to God Almighty are the destinations of conservatism.

True conservatives hold firm to their social values, which to the world are social ills.

They uphold their Victorian principles. They are judgmental, but they judge right from wrong, truth from lies, and moral from immoral. Conservatives sing from the same hymn sheet. There are no differences between a conservative from Liverpool in Great Britain and a conservative from Missouri in the United States. Conservatives might not sing the same tune but "Abide with me" is "Abide with me." And it goes without saying that they forbid gay marriage and abortion.

The conservatism ideology lifts all boats; conservatism knows no bias, it is all about the truth. Conservatism will convert people one way or another. Conservatism has its resemblance to the Gospel; it is the sister ideology to the Word of God. Therefore, conservatism is the cutting edge ideology for all humanity. Any other ideology is an endorsement from Satan on a quest to make it to Heaven. But it depends on the stamp of approval from Satan. An ideology like liberalism is an ideology that has not only been endorsed by Satan but rubberstamped, idea-driven, and for the most part, taken over by Satan himself.

Conservatism is ageless. Conservatism is about maintaining the status quo—the tradition of marriage, the sanctity of life, and the tradition of the family—while other ideologies are attempting fervently to change the status quo to their own absurd and corrupt ideas. God never changes and conservatism stems from the Word of God. The Gospel answered all the questions in the world. Christianity has lost it flavor; it has lost it salt; it has been watered-down. The Gospel is the only doctrine or ideology that is perfect and impeccable; it answers the question of salvation. The Gospel and the grace of God are the only tickets to Heaven that are available. We are living in the dispensation of grace. Certain works of conservatism and Christianity will be saved, and certain works of conservatism and Christianity will be saved as if coming out of the fire, but only the Gospel preached by Jesus is guaranteed salvation for Man. Any ideology and religion that doesn't believe that Jesus is the Son of God will culminate in Hades. Hence, none of those works will be saved.

There is a marked difference between conservatism and other political ideologies. Communism, liberalism, socialism, etc. all have something in common. The common denominator is the total control of the masses; the absolute control of the citizens. On the other hand, conservatism treasures freedom for people to pursue their dreams freely. Conservatism has nothing in common with any other earthly ideology; conservatism is in a league of its own. Giving alms to the needy but not letting your left hand know what your right hand has done—that is the wholesome description of a typical God-fearing conservative. Conservatives won't support the cause of the poor in the open but in private they do. Talk is cheap; hence, conservatives don't talk the talk in the public but they walk the walk in private. Conservatives don't seek fame and glory. Human nature has been defiled by the false, flawed ideology of liberalism, Marxism, communism, socialism, etc. Conservatism is the common sense human nature of Man.

I'm gratified for true social conservatives; they are the real Christians—the Sean Hannitys, the Rick Santoroms, and the Sarah Palins of the world. They are the disciples of Jesus. They are the holy sinners. Conservatives will forever have the bully pulpit to espouse the truth; they are guided by the Spirit of Truth Himself. Thank God for the true conservatives who are for all intents and purposes God's reserve. Sean Hannity said, "Teach them how to fish rather than giving them a fish every day of their life until you run out of fish." Conservatives want to teach you how to be independent; God didn't give Israel manna forever.

God made me a conservative. My lifestyle is conservatism. I often wonder how I lived a conservative lifestyle without any planning. I lived a conservative life without knowing it, and once I realized it, I thanked God. It gives me joy to ascertain that I innocently lived a conservative life without any forethoughts or pre-knowledge. Being conservative is just how God created me to be; it's inherent in me; it's just who I'm. So I am not loco when I lambaste abortionists and gay marriage activists. There is nothing manufactured about my stance on conservatism.

I'm a dyed-in-the-wool conservative. I'm to the right of Rick Santorum; no man is to the right of me. If you see me, Nndy Nenty, you have seen Rush Limbaugh; but if you see Rush Limbaugh, you have seen conservatism. If you see Jesus Christ you have seen God, but if you see God Almighty you have seen eternal life. Conservatism is ageless because it stems from the Word of God.

Now the rest of the acts of Sean Hannity, and what he did, and his leadership, are they not written in *Deliver Us from Evil: Defeating Terrorism, Despotism, and Liberalism*?

Now the rest of the acts of Tom DeLay, and his leadership and his fights against enemies in the U.S. House, are they not written in *No Retreat, No Surrender: One American's Fight*?

Now the rest of the acts of Rick Santorum, and his leadership, and all that he did in the U.S. Senate, are they not written in *It Takes a Family: Conservatism and the Common Good*?

Now the rest of the acts of Mark Levine, and the conservative manifesto, are they not written in *Ameritopia: The Unmaking of America*?

Now the rest of the acts of Sarah Palin, her rise to prominence, and her fights against the establishment, are they not written in *Going Rogue: An American Life*?

Now the rest of the acts of Michelle Malkin, are they not written in *Unhinged: Exposing Liberals Gone Wild*?

Gun Ownership

On the gun ownership front, I'm a conservative who is against conservatism.

I was once against gun ownership but as I became more learned on the Holy Scriptures, I reluctantly joined the conservative platform on gun ownership. And I forgo my personal bias to tow the line and accept the Republican notion of gun ownership. But personally I'm against the ownership of guns in any way, shape, or form. However, when Christ told His disciples to take up weapons with them, then that made me think twice on my anti-gun ownership stance.

My advice for those gun owners is that in a situation when you unload, don't shoot to kill—shoot to injure or disable, but not to kill—because the Word of God says, "Thou shalt not kill." Save during war time, any Man that kills an intruder is guilty of murder and the full weight of God's judgment will be upon that individual. A thief in your home is not war time, so to murder a thief in the name of self-defense is a grave act that in no way, shape, or form is acceptable before God Almighty. The word of God has not condoned self-defense. So that is where I part company with conservatism.

I wouldn't dispute conservatives on gun ownership because Christ authorized His disciples to carry weapons with them. God has appointed those dressed to kill. And those are the ones in the military. They are the only ones exempt from murder.

If you gunned down a thief for the sake of self—defense, God will say, "I sent a thief to your house and you killed my servant." Then what will be your reply? The only defense to murdering a fellow human being is if it were an accident. Shooting an intruder is not accidental; you knew exactly what your intentions were. The only murdering that will be forgiven is if it was done in innocence; it wasn't premeditated, hence you didn't intend to kill that clay that God made, such as in a car accident. But removing the firearm out of its sheath and pulling the trigger is not unforeseen. You knew what you were doing, thus God will judge you as a murderer. And there wouldn't be any difference between you and a mass murderer. Life is not fair but the Word of God is truth. Should you murder an intruder; the blood of that thief that you slay will be upon your head. And that blood will be chomping at the bit to judge you on the day of Reckoning. The truth will always be hard to swallow.

There is a certain degree of ignorance; an ugliness for someone to own a gun for the sake of self-defense. There is something sinister about owning a firearm for protection's sake. It's common sense to own a firearm for self-defense, but it's not common sense to pull the trigger for the kill. There is no common sense nor wisdom in killing a creature that God created in His own image.

In New York, fugitively speaking, there is an infrared beam on everyone's forehead. You get accustomed to it; hence you walk with caution. Even babies get hit with stray bullets. Thank God for London, in the United Kingdom, where even the law enforcement doesn't possess a gun. How refreshing is London, where guns are forbidden?

If you cite Man's law in order to support a murderer whose murdering doesn't affect your household, then you have to also cite Man's law if the murderer killed your offspring, lest you make a hypocrite of yourself. You can't have it both ways. You can't, in the name of self—defense, support a murderer today but tomorrow condemn the murderer because it affected you in some way. That is pure hypocrisy. Jesus Christ said do unto others as you wished done to you.

There is nothing fortuitous about self-defense murder. Upholding the gun ownership law is an Achilles heel for conservatism. The wisdom of conservatism ends in the upholding of gun ownership. For those who believe in the ownership of guns for self-defense—regardless of the potential loss of life—that is the end of conservatism. You are at your own peril if you own a gun in the name of self-defense.

It's not about the beginning, it is about the end. The man was a murderer. Whatever he did that was notable prior to murdering was just a dry run leading to the act of murdering. If my daughter is pregnant then she must conceive the baby because if I suffer her to abort the baby, then doesn't that make me a hypocrite? Before you take the leap and support the defense of a murderer in the name of self-defense, put yourself in the shoes of the victim's bereaved family and ask yourself if you will have the same opinion if the person killed was your offspring? Would you have the same conviction? If you truly certainly have the same opinion, then your righteousness is not of this world. But if you have a change of mind, then you have lot of work to do. If I believe in self-defense that might lead to murdering, that means that my wisdom has come to an end. That is where I part company with conservatives who believe in gun ownership for the express purpose of self-defense.

Liberalism

I will disagree to an extent with fellow conservatives, but with liberals we disagree indefinitely. No middle or common ground absolutely. We disagree to disagree; we don't agree, period, so as to avoid cutting ties in the future.

I don't want my intelligence being insulted. So I don't deal personally with liberals.

It's nauseating to listen to liberal's ideals and policies. It really does put a bad taste in my mouth regardless of how profoundly spiritual I am. If you stomach liberalism, then you certainly stomach what is nauseating. It's imperative for liberal policies to be regurgitated. Listening to liberals and liberalism makes me mentally sick. I don't have the patience to hearken to partial truths or half-truths, which are everything but the truth; I don't have the patience to hearken to lies.

I consider liberals as dead weights, especially those who are ignorant. I consider seasoned liberals as diabolic practitioners involved in idolatry. I love my people like I'm supposed to, although most of them happened to be liberals. Every now and then I have to lambaste my people with the view that they will convert. And it hits me where it hurts to chide my own people. That is when it really gets difficult, if I have to berate my own people.

I don't know how to communicate with liberals. They are the scarlet letter of this adulterous generation. I have ignorantly liked some liberals in the past; would to God it wasn't so, but I won't condemn the past. I stand firmly in my belief that liberals are the uprights of Satan disguised as an angel. By and large they are being used hook, line, and sinker by the Devil. They might be ignorant but it's because they are devoid of wisdom and understanding. They allowed themselves to be indoctrinated, and hence are reprobates for Satan. They are undertaking the Devil's bidding.

Seasoned liberals are the prominent, the scholars, union rank and file, and the politicians; they are the brain of liberalism.

Ignorant liberals are tools for seasoned liberals. They carry the devil's water without knowing it; they are the muscle of liberalism. Liberal captives are predominately African Americans and Hispanics. They are prisoners to liberalism; they have been held captive and in hostage, so they are unable to challenge the status quo. They are held captive in the form of incentives and welfare which they are afforded by the crafty policies of the seasoned liberals. These liberal captives rubberstamp liberal policies without critical thinking.

Liberals see to it that you remain wards of the state, which in turn does little in the way of dependency. Liberals' clients are the true definition of stagnant water; they are dead weights to the country. Rush Limbaugh said about liberalism, "It's the most gutless choice you can make." A liberal's worst nightmare would be for you to break the glass ceiling; they don't want you to be independent. "They need a permanent underclass of dependent people," Rush concluded. On one hand, liberals are snakes in the grass. On the other hand, liberals are white sepulchers and white-washed walls. There is nothing substantive about liberalism; hence, they are wells without water.

Liberalism is an ideology that is godless and sinister but is dressed up under the guise of fairness, innocence, help, progress, care, concern, friendship, and inequality. Everything liberals do is under this guise. Communism, totalitarianism, statism, etc. are of a kindred spirit with liberalism.

With liberals you can't win—no matter how blatantly the truth stares in their faces. No matter how valid your argument is, they wouldn't retreat or yield; they will keep coming up with their false premises. And before you know it, bystanders will not be capable of distinguishing between you and a liberal, thereby labeling the dissenters as fools.

Trying to convince a liberal of the truth is fighting a losing battle. The bottom line is that you can't be victorious when you pit yourself against the ignorant. Ignorance dominates in an earthly, materialistic, immoral world. As a result, it's utterly difficult to proselytize liberals.

Can a liberal be a Christian? Any Man could claim to be a Christian. Liberals are the Devil's vessels; there are no two ways about it. The Devil is an agent of God, too. But let the tares grow together with the wheat; at the end of the day the Harvester will weed them out.

Liberalism parallels Satanism. Liberals are never jubilant, they are never satisfied and they remain mean-spirited. Even in their victory they remain angry. The Devil is never satisfied; he only lies in wait for those who are totally devoted to God. Liberals only slander and censure those who dare threaten and challenge their ideology.

Liberalism is nothing short of an immoral policy. The dirty laundry of liberalism is godless. It lectures a five-year-old about sex education. It lectures a ten-year-old on how to use a condom. These liberals abolished the Lord's prayers from school curriculum.

Liberalism is the freebies ideology. They live by the gravy train. They deceive people in the name of welfare and entitlements, etc. Perpetual entitlement fuels the gravy train. According to Limbaugh, "Every demand" has a "Christmas morning." African Americans and Hispanics feel entitled to their demands. Liberalism causes Man to be wards of the state.

When did reality become synonymous with fantasy? Liberalism makes you believe that utopia is reality. Utopia is nothing but fantasy._You have to eat with a long spoon when dealing with seasoned liberals. Don't find common ground with the Devil and his liberal disciples.

For the liberal captives, government is the limit. For the so-called disadvantaged, the thirsty and the hungry, the sky is no longer the limit—rather welfare benefits and freebies are the limit. The government benefits which they appropriate every given period couldn't be any better. They long to be wards of the state. Government is their god. Government is their one and only, their be-all and end-all, their cradle and their grave, and their utopia.

Liberals refer to themselves as "progressive" because they recognize that the term "liberal" has a bad connotation. Itinerant Jewish exorcists who deceived the public in the days of the Apostle Paul are no different from liberals. They keep muddying the waters.

Does a fish know he is in water? Do liberals know they live on everything but the truth? Liberalism is predicated on a false premise; it is predicated on lies, demagogy, prevarication, and the whole nine yards.

Certain of the seasoned liberals are the epitome of hypocrisy; they preach in support of gay marriage, abortion, etc., but in their household they practice not what they preach. Their message is only intended for the liberal captives, to win their votes and their support. In reality, they don't want any part of what they preach in public; for them, power trumps truth. Liberal policies take advantage of the disadvantaged.

Why do liberals breathe out cruelty against the rich? It's simply because most of their constituents are destitute. And yet they have filthy rich liberals among their constituents, but those are exempt. And because conservatism stands in their way of entrenching power, they wish the worst case scenario for conservatives.

Liberalism is all about amassing power; it's all about doing everything within reach to appropriate power. They are power hungry. And as such, through lies and deceitful means, they brainwash and indoctrinate minorities.

Social inequality is the biggest liberal crusade. Liberals fight tooth and nail to condemn and excoriate the rich. Remember the written Word of God says in Proverbs 23 verse 5 and Matthew 19 verse 24, "For riches certainly make themselves wings; they fly away as an eagle toward heaven." And Jesus said, "It is easier for a camel to go through the eye of a needle, than for a rich Man to enter into the kingdom of God." So why do liberals condemn the wealthy when Jesus has already put a curse on the rich? Anyone that condemns the rich is trying to outmaneuver the curse Jesus rested on the rich. Christ Himself had ties with the rich. One of Christ's disciples was a tax collector. He was wealthy before he became Christ's disciple. Nicodemus was also a rich Pharisee who associated with Christ. The rich men that Christ talked about were the ones who inherit riches from their fore-fathers and their fathers—those who were born with a silver spoon in their mouth. But those who work righteously and achieve the wealth through their sweat and tears are blessed by God; they are not the rich people of the world but they are the rich people of God. For instance, Rush Limbaugh and Sean Hannity went through hell in order to be successful in this life. Rush Limbaugh was fired seven times before his work finally became a memorial before God. Hannity pound the pavement day in and day out and worked in armpit places until he relocated to Georgia where God kept him a favorable position, and from then onwards the rest is history, as both Rush Limbaugh and Sean Hannity are the most popular names in

America because they were steadfast and devoted in what they desired. They kept their eyes on the prize and all of a sudden they have the most enviable jobs in the whole country and it is nothing but the working of the Lord.

Seasoned liberals own the skin color of Blacks. Since one's ideology is not written in the forehead as one's skin color is, Blacks are generally perceived as liberals. That is the perspective. Seasoned liberals stereotype Blacks by their skin color. If certain Blacks are conservative, they automatically will be behind enemy lines. And they will be raked over the coals for daring to differ from liberalism. So conservatism is an escape from the general perspective. So being a Black conservative, the opponents will be taken aback for that reason and they will be grouped differently.

The gravy train will never leave the station as far as the liberals are concerned. If you go after the crown jewel, their *pièce de résistance*, their entitlements, the reason why they exist, then you become enemy number one. Everyday has to be Christmas morning in order for liberalism to be espoused; hence, utopia is every day for liberals. Race-baiters, abortionists, homosexual marriage proponents, blasphemers, idolaters, etc.—choose your name for liberals. African American and Hispanic conservatives quickly become the elephant in the room and the enemy of the state because they differ from liberalism. As much as I hate evil, I hate the liberal ideology itself. The notion of a colorblind society is an enemy to liberalism. And liberalism has brainwashed Blacks into believing that a colorblind society is a scheme pioneered by conservatives. Hence the notion that colorblindness is an enemy to Blacks too.

Liberals wants to split the baby, while conservatives dare not. Liberals can't accept defeat; their exclusive desire is to split the baby. Conservatives want to preserve the nation; they don't want the baby to be split. Liberals want to dismantle this great county. Liberalism hankers to shatter Christianity, marriage traditions, the traditional family, moral values, social values, and capitalism. Liberalists designed their own version of freedom, which is freedom without responsibility. Hence, freedom for abortion is one of their main agendas. Liberals are crap in a bucket; they are the biggest strangers to the truth because there is no truth in them. The abject truth to liberalism is like showing the cross to Dracula. "East is East and West is West, and never the twain shall meet." While liberalism is predicated on lies and falsehood, conservatism is based on nothing but the absolute truth. Liberals preach fairness. Conservatives recognize that we all have different lots in life. Liberals want to manage one's lot in life. Conservatism is all about maintaining morals, values, and traditions. Both Liberalism and conservatism preach freedom; but conservatism preaches freedom that comes with judgment and penalty. Liberalism preaches freedom without virtues.

While failure is an orphan and success has many fathers, conservatism doesn't brand failures; conservatism affords one all the opportunity in the world that one requires. You own your destiny. Liberalism brands failures; liberalism limits your dreams in life and sets in place policies to control your destiny. Everything about liberalism is made up out of whole cloth.

I don't uphold or believe in fairness, entitlement and welfare; I don't also support abortion and gay marriage. They are all part and parcel of liberalism.

Abortion

Liberalists support abortion. Liberalists condone and facilitate abortion. An act of abortion is an act of murder, pure and simple. No ifs, ands, or buts. And the Word of God states time and time again, "Thou shalt not kill." I'm hook, line, and sinker against abortion. The fact that I'm talking about abortion means that I have to circumvent sex only after marriage.

Who is considered a living being? The Almighty God said He knew the prophet Jeremiah even before Jeremiah was formed in his mother's womb. And Almighty God said He sanctified Jeremiah when he was in his mother's womb. And to boot, Jacob and Esau were both in their mother's womb and the Bible said they were vying for supremacy in their mother Rebecca's womb. So this idea that an unborn child who is aborted, should not be counted in "thou shalt not kill" is absurd to the worst degree.

I won't for a minute relax my view on abortion. Even if it hits close to home; even if it hits inside of home. Why do liberals aid and abet abortion? Because a vast majority of their culprits are impoverished minorities which are also their main constituents.

As a social value conservative, I am not only against abortion but I'm against sex before marriage. A staunch conservative will advocate against abortion but I will advocate against fornication or sex before marriage. Jesus Christ my Lord advocated that even looking at a woman with lust in one's heart is fornication and adultery in itself. No human being can be to the right of Jesus Christ.

Homosexual Marriage

It's one thing for men of the cloth to usher in gays into their congregation, but it's another thing for these men of the cloth to performed homosexual marriage ceremonies in their churches. These men of the cloth are playing the "all things to all men" card by accommodating homosexual couples into their congregation; they are looking down the barrel of utter domination. "Mama never said there will be days like this."

The love between two faggots or between two lesbians is not love from God; it is satanic love; it is love from the depth of hell. The Devil's scheme and object with homosexuality is to mislead the Christians into believing that supporting gay marriage is moral; thereby taking them off the right path of God. Whatever God does, Satan has his own duplicate.

There is no common sense in gay marriage; it's not logical; it's nonsense. And I'm taking no prisoners. If God forbid I had an offspring that is homosexual? No, I won't raise a kid to make it to hell. So that offspring of mine must liberate that homosexual spirit of Satan.

The Almighty God destroyed one city because of homosexuality. God Almighty knew this day would come when America would condone gay marriage, so what happened at Sodom and Gomorrah is a forerunner to what will also befall America.

If any Man supports homosexual marriage, they are gay marriage sympathizers; they are sympathizing with Satan himself. Conservatives are not against homosexuals; conservatives are against any principle that goes against the tradition and tenets of marriage as defined by the Word of God.

Jesus said Man should multiply, so homosexual so-called marriage is wrong beyond measure. To even try to argue for gay marriage is an abomination in itself.

I'm observing why the new version or interpretation of the Bible hasn't erased or significantly modified the verse that condemns homosexuals as an abomination.

I'm not homophobic by any stretch of the imagination because I can't abhor what God created, even though homosexuality is satanic. So I'm reduced to being a perpetually blunt instrument against homosexuality.

African American issues

Lincoln freed the slaves by essentially giving the White slave owners incentives. Blacks, all they were desirous for was their freedom. Lincoln oversaw the emancipation because he had a good heart. Franklin Delano Roosevelt, (FDR) on the other hand, gave Blacks incentives just to win their votes and to win them to the Democratic Party; hence, welfare programs were established. So would Blacks rather have their liberation or incentives? That is the million-dollar question. Because for all intents and purposes, the Blacks should be mostly Republican, because it was the Republicans that granted them freedom, not the Democrats. It was these Democrats that were against Lincoln's application for emancipating the slaves. And these same Democrats sent FDR to sympathize on their behalf, and as such, throw the Blacks a bone. And FDR threw bones to the Blacks, and henceforth they all with one accord joined the Democratic Party and abandoned the Republican Party, which was the pioneer that led to their emancipation.

So one can safely conclude that Blacks value incentives more than they value freedom. You can't have it both ways. Republicans could only grant you the freedom for which many of you for decades have died. And the last words of most of the Blacks who couldn't witness the day that they were freed were, "Keep fighting; don't give up." But while men slept, here come the Democrats, who came in the middle of the night and planted the tares among the wheat. They corrupted the minds of Blacks with incentives like welfare programs, etc. And then Blacks abandoned the hand that fed them as they unanimously threw the Republican Party down under the bus and eventually alienated, and cast their lots with the Democratic Party. Hence the words of their fathers and forefathers became worthless. How long will the African American community be in the wilderness?

How long will African Americans pledge allegiance to the Democratic Party? A party that for all intents and purposes considers African Americans as pitiful, witless victims.

In every generation, the African American community has been reaping the whirlwind solely because they chose rather to sow the wind. Why are over forty-three percent of African American babies being aborted in this generation? And why are over seventy-three percent of African American babies born out of wedlock? It's the most amazing thing that in this generation there are more Black babies born into single-parent households than married-couple households.

All my diverse acquaintances know I loathe the attitudes of African Americans; it goes without saying. My dislike for Blacks is not manufactured. So I wouldn't blame myself, rather I blame the Potter. But wasn't Christ accursed with despising the stiff-necked attitude of the Jews?

It was the Black president of America that caused America to transgress in the act of endorsing, supporting, and rubberstamping homosexual marriage. It justifies my dislike for the race as a whole. The abortion rate in the Black population can't be compared to the abortion rate of other races. That statistic further justifies my disdain for the race. Unwed parents, teenage pregnancy, Black illiteracy rate, Black incarceration, and recidivate rates are just other justifiers.

The reason why I detest the attitudes of African Americans is because I want them to change their attitudes and know that life is not about White or Black but about right or wrong, moral or immoral, virtue or vice; this life is about God Almighty. If I profess adoration for the African American community, that means that I support race-baiting; that means I have no qualms about the high rate of abortion; that means that I condone the high rate of unwed parents and other legends within the African American community. These staple issues within the African American community need to be rectified. I won't live a lie. I won't lie to myself just to please African Americans; right is right and wrong is wrong. Hence, if I say I admire the African American community that means that I love the wrongs; that means that I love the immoral.

If I condemn African Americans it's solely because I want them to change. Saying nothing about their reprehensible ways does little in the way of change; it doesn't do any good. But reprimanding them untowardly will make them think twice and will go a long way toward purity and cleansing within the African American community. I could take pleasure in shooting from the hip ceaselessly at man, but at the end of the day, all I want is for man to repent.

At the end of the day, I don't like Black people. At the end of the day, I am a conservative—that is what people are going to remember about me. He was a Christian but he flocked to Rush Limbaugh, etc. He was a nice person, we respected him, and liked him, but Nndy didn't like Black people.

America, Downward Spiral

When will America no longer be the land of the free and home of the brave? America was founded as a capitalist, God-fearing country, but liberals for decades have done their level best to Europeanize, Africanize, and Asianize the country.

I was buried in politics and it culminated with a degree in political science. I was married to American politics for years but I forced out a divorce. I couldn't continue to stomach the shenanigans and the moral corruptions that were taking place on Capitol Hill.

I have risen above American politics. If Obama becomes ruler of America forever I wouldn't care a hill of beans because there is no more respect and honor for the White House office. I don't imagine why any conservative should even run for the Oval Office. If caution is not taken, woe would be unto any conservative Republican who attempts to run for office. The dignity for the White House is gone; it has been tarnished for good. Any immoral ideologue and demagogue whose elevator doesn't reach the top floor can rule this once great country.

My disillusionment with politics is not merely with the White House but with the United States Congress too. The United States Senate stinks. I was revolted and utterly gutted at the fall of the U.S. Congress. It's a crying shame what has befallen the U.S. Congress. The moral purists who should uphold the tenets of morality have had their clocks cleaned by the perverse bunch in federal elections, and hence, have been thrown out of Congress. I'm contented that Rick Santorum and Tom DeLay are no longer on Capitol Hill. Gone are the days when American politics was the be-all and the end-all.

Perhaps it's because I live a spiritual life and I see things spiritually, not earthly. Churches are filled with gay marriage and abortion activists. It will never be the same. And that is just a microcosm of what has befallen this great country. Conservatives should just hold on to their conservative ideology and beliefs, but most importantly hold on to their faith in the Heavenly Father because the time to hold on to their country has been overtaken. The country has been overtaken by those with reprobate minds and it starts at the top of the food chain; it starts at the White House on down to Congress and down to the states, etc. The country will forever be in a downward spiral.

America didn't originate from itself. It originated from the Brits. The Brits are original. Conservatives all across the fruited plain should separate themselves from the reprobate minds; those who are programmed by Satan and his kingdom. Again I stress, trying to capture the White House and Congress is fighting a losing battle, solely because of the country's acute immoral problems.

Moral corruption has taken up residence in the White House and in the US Congress.

The White House has been tarnished and defiled. George Bush was the last honorable ruler, but he himself was also stained from the whoredom cesspool that has corrupted the country. A White House, a Congress, and a State that endorses gay marriage and abortion are doomed. Every kingdom must fall and the American kingdom is on the verge. Armageddon and the apocalypse are on the verge of rearing their ugly heads. It's not a question of if or when America will fall, it is a question of how drastic will it be. The only silver lining is the grace of God, but what should happen in the meanwhile? Conservatives have to maintain their unshakable faith in God Almighty while the liberals rearrange the decks chairs on the sinking Titanic.

A time will come when any American born could become a United States president. Obama is not fit to tie the shoelace of a certain Rush Limbaugh. There is no more dignity and morale in the office of the president. Any American could be president. A gay activist could be an American president. A womanizer could be an American president; a staunch supporter of abortion could be an American president. A race-baiter could be an American president; enough said.

Can a Man with morals marry a prostitute? Because of liberalism, America has been married to a prostitute. Should a Man marry a fellow Man? Because of liberalism, America has committed the greatest of all abominations. Satan's wishes have all come true. America loss its virginity in 2007 when Senator Rick Santorum and Majority Leader DeLay vacated the United States Congress. Their departures mark the end of morality in the United States Congress. But imagine a woman that participates in fornication and whoredom every day for six straight years. Unfortunately, that is the story of the great United States of America.

Once Satan takes over, the Spirit of God will depart. Light cannot coexist with darkness. You can't serve God and mammon. But America has chosen to serve the latter. People express their desire for Obama to be president for life. And I wouldn't object to their desire because Obama was chosen by the dark-side, and the American people will feel the darkness.

So long as my fellow conservatives are fine, dandy, and untainted, my prayer goes out to them. I couldn't even pretend to care if America is destroyed by earthquakes, hurricanes, or volcanos in diverse places. But one thing I know for sure is that God will not suffer His people to die like chickens. And who are God's people? The true unabashed conservatives and Christians who practice what they preach. Conservatives are not going to come home to roost.

The Gospel According to Obama

The ruler of America, Barack Obama, has the biggest bully pulpit in the world. As an ultra-conservative, I'm a critic of Obama and I will be lying to Satan if I agreed that Obama has done an awesome job as president of America.

The world claimed and believed that Obama has compassion for the downtrodden, etc.

If you put lipstick on a pig, at the end of the day that pig is still a pig. If you put a black skin on Satan because he shows compassion to people, at the end of the day Satan is still the Devil. Peter showed compassion to Jesus when Jesus told His disciples of His anticipated death. Yet Satan used Peter to show compassion to Jesus. The Devil can also be friendly, but at the end his perceived friendliness will be severe antagonism.

Matthew 16:21-23 states:

From that time forth began Jesus to shew unto his disciples, how that he must go unto Jerusalem, and suffer many things of the elders and chief priests and scribes, and be killed, and be raised again the third day. Then Peter took him, and began to rebuke him, saying, "Be it far from thee, Lord: this shall not be unto thee." But he turned, and said unto Peter, "Get thee behind me, Satan: thou art an offence unto me: for thou savourest not the things that be of God, but those that be of men."

Obama pontificates about being one's brother's keeper, yet he has a half-brother living in abject poverty in Africa. Obama might as well wish his brother dead. After Cain killed Abel, God asked Cain of the whereabouts of his slain brother Abel. And what was Cain's response? "Am I my brother's keeper?" This same ruler of America on numerous occasions supported infanticide (botched abortions.) That means even when the fetus survived the abortion, Obama still championed against the survival of the born-alive infant. Even when God saved the fetus the first time from dying, men sought that the born-alive infant must by any means necessary be brought to death. Isn't Obama heartless? It's the most amazing thing. Isn't it ghastly and gruesome that aborted babies born alive are put to the sword? How grotesque is it for liberals to support botched and partial-birth abortion?

Obama publicly endorsed homosexual marriage; hence, all the Americans who supported and cast their lot for Obama have also aided and abetted homosexual marriage. Obama, the American ruler who endorsed same-sex marriage has already done the irreversible worst by advocating for homosexual marriage; any criticism leveled against him is justified. A limb for limb criticism against Obama is justified; it doesn't need to be analyzed because Obama has done the worst. Sanctioning homosexual marriage is the worst of all the abominations. Even if a lie is told about Obama, I would support the premise of the lie.

Obama, the American ruler who rubberstamped abortion reckons that teenage pregnancy is someone being "punished with a baby." There is no end in sight to this immoral gospel according to Obama.

Obama is a forerunner of the antichrist. Of course he must profess Christianity in order to infiltrate and destroy Christianity from within rather than from without. He would, in attempting to destroy Christianity, be from the outside looking in if he professed to be of any other religion.

Obama supported gay marriage in Africa and then said "God bless" Planned Parenthood—an organization that solely champions and facilitates abortion. Obama is an agent of Satan the Devil. And you have Louis Farrakhan calling the White man the "devil," and millions of African Americans concur with Farrakhan. The real devils are the Black leaders like Obama. Let him hold up a mirror to himself and realize that he is the devil's numero uno servant.

Obama savors to do the things of Man and not the things of God. He endorsed gay marriage but he is heterosexual—that makes him a hypocrite. He said "God bless" Planned Parenthood, using God's name in vain. He toured Africa and pleaded for Africans to legalize homosexual marriage; Obama in so doing exposed his true colors, which are longed etched in stone. Obama championing the legalization of gay marriage in Africa means that Americans can't overlook what he did in America in endorsing gay marriage. It proves that his initial support was genuine. You can't say Obama did so solely to win votes, you can't say it was an oversight on Obama's part, and you can't give him the benefit of the doubt, because if Obama endorsed gay marriage in America solely to win votes, he wouldn't have dare requested Africa to legalize homosexuality and then move to cut off funds to countries that refuse to adhere and comply with his request. If you endorse homosexual marriage and practice heterosexuality, then you are a hypocrite.

You have Jamie Foxx calling Obama personal "lord and savior." Certain African American leaders need to hold a mirror to themselves to realize who the real devil is. Obama's immoral policies are just the tip of the iceberg. Liberals treat them as if they're nothing to write home about—as if nothing is new since Genesis. But it was the tip of the iceberg that sank the Titanic on its voyage to New York from Southampton, and how many casualties were numbered after that dreadful aftermath? How many babies conceived in the womb are being aborted by policies spearheaded by Obama and godless liberals? Just as Judas was to betray Jesus, Obama was to endorse gay marriage. It's mind-boggling that Obama supports infanticide. It's just the ramification of electing a total demagogue—an empty suit—into the presidency. There is no end in sight of the liberals' rationalized immoral policies.

Power behind the Throne

Power of the tongue overrides the power of the world. Jesus had power by the words He spoke; the words He spoke were the Word of God Himself. Pontius Pilate had the power of the world because he was elected into office.

When I saw Rush Limbaugh, I experienced his power and his influence, and you instantly know that this is someone that God created. If Rush has all this power, splendor, and respect, then what about God Himself, where all powers belong to Him? Everything about Rush is real. So his presence was real. The power that Obama has is an authoritarian power. Obama doesn't possess the power of the word because he is unauthentic. Obama has the power of a pharaoh and that of Pontius Pilate. Rush has the power of a Jesus-like figure in the sense that it was the word that Jesus spoke that made Him a King. It's the word out of Rush Limbaugh's mouth that makes him the most powerful figure in America, save for the American President. Rush Limbaugh's power is based on immeasurable commonsense ideas; liberals and the opposition place the lion's share of blame on Rush for the political gridlock in the country. Rush said, "My power is placed next to his [Obama]. He says I'm the reason he can't move his agenda. The media accepts that, takes it forward and proceeds to rip me and so forth."

No Man can hold a candle to Rush Limbaugh—whether Pope John Paul II, Martin Luther King, John F. Kennedy, Margret Thatcher, Nelson Mandela, Abraham Lincoln, Ronald Reagan, or Wilson Churchill, etc. Except for Martin Luther King, all these great names were elected into office. Therefore they are all pharaohs; they are all Pontius Pilates. They have the authoritarian power of Pilate to crucify the Son of God, but outside their authoritarian power they are average Joes. On the other hand, Rush Limbaugh and Martin Luther King are Jesus-Christ-like figures. They were not elected into office like the aforementioned names. It is the power of their tongue; it is the word that proceeds out of their mouth that placed them a cut above others. Christ has the power by the words He spoke.

Excluding the president of America, Rush Limbaugh has been the most powerful person in America for over two decades now. It's no mean feat. And once presidents of America abdicate their office, their authoritarian power ceases. They become forgotten figures. Martin Luther King was powerful, too, because of the words that he spoke. Blacks and minorities for years idolized Martin Luther King, and there seems to be no end of singing Martin Luther King's praises. But it is said in many quarters that Martin Luther King didn't believe that Jesus was the Son of God. Whether it is true or not, the fact that there was some degree of doubt that King questioned Jesus' immaculate conception and resurrection, means that his greatness ends where Rush Limbaugh's greatness begins. Rush Limbaugh truly, unequivocally believes that Jesus is the Son of God. Rush Limbaugh's father was a Gospel teacher. And Rush Limbaugh constantly defends the tenets of Jesus Christ from his bully pulpit when these tenets have been tarnished by liberals.

Idolizers and celebrity and hero worshippers should recognize that John F. Kennedy, Martin Luther King, etc. died and they didn't resurrect like Jesus Christ.

Poverty

One of liberalism main agenda is their under the guise fight against poverty. Poverty is one of the leading spirits of death. Why all of a sudden liberalism fights tooth and nail to end poverty? Why not 100 years ago? What makes this generation better than those who perished years ago due to poverty? Fighting against poverty is fighting a lose battle. So liberalism endless crusade against poverty is a vain battle as all of their other agenda are.

There are different lots in life for mankind. The spirit of poverty existed from the beginning of time and it will culminate only at the end of time. Life as a human being is about social inequality. You basically accused God or stopped short from accusing God for unfairness because there are millions of impoverished people in the world. And Man began to question the clay and Potter issue all because they want to succor the poor, the disadvantaged, aggrieved, hungry, and the thirsty.

Famine, which causes poverty, was first mentioned in the Bible in Genesis 12:10, "And there was a famine in the land: and Abram went down into Egypt to sojourn there; for the famine was grievous in the land."

Who are the poor people of the world? Because Donald Trump is a church rat compared to Bill Gates. So who are these mystical, poor, penniless people of the world? Poor people to me are the ones in Africa, Asia, etc. I'm highlighting the ones who don't have food to put on the table; the ones who eat every other day or even worst. If there are Americans with such statistics, the American government is readily available for those dire Americans who don't have bread to eat. But the corrupt government in Africa or in Asia refuses to provide or is unable to provide for its citizens.

Think of the worst that can befall those living in poverty. What Americans are experiencing and calling poverty is a fortune for those in developing countries. Wretched street beggars and the homeless are the only Americans in my book who are living in abject poverty.

I judge poverty through the lens of those living in Africa, in Asia, in Latin America, and in the Caribbean.

I'm not against public assistance but it should only be afforded to the needy, the beggars, and the homeless. There are millions of Americans who eat the bread of idleness yet they constantly jeremiad for their misfortune and for their penurious condition. Poor Americans has to be poorer or as poor as a church rat before I join the bandwagon for them to be incentivized with government handouts.

Poverty is a servant of God. It brings people closer to God. Poverty-stricken people worship God with the hope that God will answer their abject, wretched situation. So to try to fight against poverty is fighting against a great servant of God. The prevalent poverty in areas around the world transpired for God's reasons. And the Potter will care for His creatures.

In Deuteronomy 8:3, God suffered some people to hunger so "that He might make thee know that Man doth not live by bread only, but by every word that proceedeth out of the mouth of the Lord doth Man live." Hence God earmarked certain people to be poor so that men will know that Man should not live by bread alone but by every word that comes out of the mouth of God. Deuteronomy 15:11 states,

"For the poor shall never cease out of the land: therefore I command thee, saying, Thou shalt open thine hand wide unto thy brother, to thy poor, and to thy needy, in thy land."

After they coercively departed from Egypt, rather than dying in the wilderness, the Israelites questioned if there weren't enough graves in Egypt so that they could die there. So what is the difference with the Israelite outcry in the wilderness and those living in poverty in Western society?

The poor in Africa are the ones praying earnestly for the crumbs to fall off the table of the so-called poor Americans. They are praying for the crumbs to fall off the master's table. And woe to that dog or pet that will come and try to compete with the impoverished Africans who are struggling for survival. If so-called poor Americans visit Africa and witness firsthand the drastic poverty, should they return to America, they will be immeasurably grateful to God every day for the so-called poverty that they are experiencing in America. They will be content with their situation.

Does a beggar have a choice? Poverty is part and parcel of life. You can't compare a poor man in Texas to a poor man in Kenya. Poor Americans should realize that if they eat the bread of idleness, if they refuse to pull themselves up by their boot straps, if they don't pound the pavement—then they won't have a pot to piss in. They have to learn how to live within their means; it's all about learning how to adjust.

I will be demanding parity with the Almighty God should I venture to solve the dire poverty occurring in Africa, Asia, etc. Poverty has taken many lives; it is in a league of its own. Poverty will continue to be prevalent until the Apocalypse rears its ugly head. It's human nature for the poor and the needy to condemn and be jealous of the rich. But if the poor and the needy were in the shoes of the rich and became rich tomorrow, they wouldn't condemn the rich. But the poor's destitute condition comes with hatred and envy toward the rich. Christ said it will be more difficult for a rich Man to make it to Heaven than for a camel to go through the eye of a needle. So the rich Man already has a biblical challenge. If today you are poor and you wholeheartedly condemn the rich, and if tomorrow's windfall changed your fortune and you became rich, your riches would not last, because yesterday you had already condemned the rich.

Famine is a servant of God. Famine eventually culminates in poverty. Fighting against poverty is a losing battle. If you fight against famine, you are fighting against poverty. If you fight against poverty you are fighting against the Word of God.

Conservatism takes a commonsense approach to poverty. It's a losing battle to try to eliminate or eradicate poverty. Poverty is pervasive; poverty is a curse. The spirit of poverty lives as long as Man exists. Poverty is part of mankind. Rush Limbaugh once stated that there are millions of Christians in reduced circumstances worldwide who attend the tabernacle of God day in and day out, yet they still remain poor until they give up the ghost.

Because of the lack of manna, the children of Israel cried that if there wasn't enough graves in Egypt for them to be buried in Egypt rather than in the wilderness. There are enough graves in America so the poor Americans on life support would not have to resort to despair like the children of Israel did. Man shouldn't live by food alone but by every word that comes out of the mouth of the Lord.

Matthew 4 verse 4 says, "Man should not live by bread alone but by every word that proceeds out of the mouth of God." So why fight against poverty? While liberalism wants Man to live by food alone, conservatism wants Man to live by every word that comes out of the mouth of the Almighty God. In order for me to support the poor there has to be a standard, a benchmark; it has to be the last resort. Privation is part of life. The only public assistance clients that I will advocate for will be the equivalent of the poor widow in the time of Christ who gave two mites, even all that she had, in the church offering, and the poor widow in the time of Elijah who readied her last meal to eat with her son before she died. I refer 1 Kings 17:8-24 to you.

Christianity

As far as this world is concerned, Christianity is the head of all religions. Judaism was the genesis but the only true religion is Christianity. And I tell you that God was for the children of Israel (Judaism) as Jesus Christ is for the Church (Christianity). Buddhism, Muslim, etc. all emerged from Judaism, but Christianity did not emerge from Judaism. Jesus Christ, the founder and the head of Christianity was born into Judaism. Jesus's death was the beginning of

37

Christianity. His death is salvation for all of mankind. Judaism or any other religion can't save Man, only Christianity can save Man.

When I converse with a Muslim or others of different faiths, I don't try to convert them. I don't even get into religious issues with them. I don't have the patience for that. I'm doing everything to complete my mission in life, and converting Muslims, etc., is not on the menu. Part of my mission is to counsel and advise my fellow true Christians not to stray away from the tenets of Christianity. I couldn't care less about the Muslim religion and if I should try to proselytize Muslims I wouldn't be capable of delivering that message without insulting their belief, because I won't hold back, I won't compromise, I won't give them the half-truth, and I won't massage my message. There is no middle ground if it comes to preaching about Jesus Christ as the true son of God. It's either Hell Fire or Heaven, as easy as that. If you are not worshiping Jesus then you are worshiping Satan. And if you happen to insult Muslims, they are renowned for an aggravated attitude. All those unwarranted behaviors to me are ancient history. If you argue with a fool, bystanders will not know the difference. I don't want my stereotype as the epitome of the smallest minority on earth to be tarnished.

I invited an elderly colleague of mine who happened to be an orthodox Jew to church and seemingly he was fit to be tied with me. No matter how strange it is, I tell you that telling people about Jesus is not strange but it will seem to be strange, especially if the recipient is an orthodox Jew or a devout Muslim. It might be difficult to preach Jesus to an orthodox Jew but at the end of the day, what is the difference between a Jew who doesn't believe in Jesus Christ and an atheist or a heathen?

A true Christian is not a racist, chauvinist, or an anti-Semite. A true Christian doesn't race-bait against Whites or against Blacks. Christianity and those who call themselves Christians should preach against discrimination, etc. Christians should not be prejudice because the head of Christianity is Jesus Christ.

Christians who happen to be racist and chauvinist are ignorant. Some of this is due to illiteracy and some is due to the misinterpretation of the Word of God. But because God has not opened their eyes and their minds, certain of those Christians will be saved. So no matter how often they are preached to about the notion of colorblindness, it will never resonate or register. Their ears are not open so they hear but they don't understand. They are not meant to be the prudent bunch. They worship God week in and week out; their understanding of God is sufficient in their eyes and they are not willing to explore. God will only judge Man according to the degree of wisdom that He has bestowed to each and every Man.

There is a distinction between true believers and those who are Christians in name only.

Christians in name only know the truth but they refuse to let the truth set them free. Christians in name only are not part of the body of Christ.

Christians are not descendants of Abraham; Christians are descendants of Jesus Christ. How marvelous is that? What more can they ask for? But why do Christians raise their hands with those that are hell-bent on tarnishing Christianity? To be a Christian is a full-time job. The plea for Christians to be born again will always be food for thought. It's a blessing to be a Christian either by birth or by adoption. But to be born into a Christian family is the biggest gift for Man, save for Christ's coming for the remission and pardoning of the sins of Man. But those that are Christians by birth sneeze at the gift of being born into a Christian family. What would have befallen Christians if Christ obeyed Satan in his first temptation when Christ was hungry? If the Jews rejected the Samaritans, who were descendants of the Jews, then what would they do to the Gentiles? Christ said the stone which the builder rejected would be the cornerstone. The Gentiles which the Jews rejected would be Christ-like.

Christ said if the Jews refuse to praise Him, He is able to raise up stones to praise Him. That is why Christians (Gentiles) are renowned for worshiping the Holy name of God Almighty.

Apostle Excel declared that the stones which Satan urged Jesus to turn to bread are the Gentiles. Satan was desirous for Jesus to turn stone to bread. Satan wanted Jesus to turn the stone (the Gentiles) to bread (to be consumed), so that the Gentiles would not have a road to salvation. But thank God for Jesus. Christians who worship God should be aware that God knows who the true believers are. The best thing in life is to worship God.

There is no convenient time to worship God; you must buy time to worship God. And the time must be off your leisure time.

If Christians seldom pray to God Almighty then they are not true believers of God. If Christians attend church service once in a blue moon or only on ceremonial days, especially if church is in close proximity, how can they justify that they are Christ-like? And certain Christians believe that it's not necessary to attend church in order to justify that they are Christians. But Christ constantly went in and out of the temple; Christ set the standard on how Christians should live their life. Christ led by example. Christ is the head of the Church so the Church has to be maintained with tithes and offerings. And Christians shouldn't judge how the tithes and the offering are being used by the men of the cloth because judgment will start from the Church. The full weight of God's judgment will be upon any corrupt man of the cloth.

There are thousands of phony men of the cloth who have by and large blasphemed against God the Holy Spirit yet they still seek God to forgive them. They have for all intents and purposes called Jesus a liar. Men of the cloth shouldn't be involved in internecine war among each other. When Angel Lucifer left Heaven, he left with one third of the angels. When men of the cloth of the same denomination fight among themselves, they leave unceremoniously to establish their own sect and they leave with a significant portion of the former congregation.

For the issue of fornication and adultery, Christ was to the right of the Almighty God. In order words, the Gospel was to the right of the Old Testament. Radioactive issues like fornication and adultery are extreme Christian issues that men of the cloth wouldn't touch with a ten-foot pole because of the fear of losing their audience and their members. Some of them are guilty because their own households are filthy, so they would rather not preach what they don't practice.

Christians who profess to love Jesus Christ but don't love their fellow Christian brethren are lying to themselves. They are not upholding the tenets of Christianity. It's only a hypocrite that professes love for Jesus who he can't see and behold, yet doesn't love the same people that Jesus has put along his way that he sees and beholds with his necked eyes. Hypocrites of the darkest characters; they pray as if everything depends on God yet they act as if everything depends on them. Their hypocrisy only serves to belittle the name of Jesus.

Rush Limbaugh and Sean Hannity audiences are in the millions, compared to the audiences of men of cloth, which are in the hundreds. Although Limbaugh and Hannity largely discuss politics, one mention of the belief in Jesus Christ and God Almighty—which they do weekly from their bully pulpit—reaches over thirty million Americans. Rush Limbaugh is a greater preacher than most of these so-called men of the cloth. Rush preached without taking any prisoners against abortion, gay marriage, fornication, etc. But legions of these so-called men of the cloth can't afford to lose their members, so they will decline talking about morality and moral decline, etc. Going in, they are already looking down the barrel of wretchedness and bareness, so immoral issues will be radioactive; it wouldn't sit well with them. They preach to the choir on uncontroversial topics. It's the height of hypocrisy.

Now the principles and values of Rush Limbaugh, are they not written in "The Way Things Ought to Be?"

Now the rest of the acts of Sean Hannity, and the conservative manifesto, are they not written in *Let Freedom Ring: Winning the War of Liberty over Liberalism?*

Thank goodness for Martin Luther, because worshiping God in the Catholic fashion is a joke compared to the way Pentecostals worship God. Christians have to dance and rejoice for God like King David did. That is what moved God; God loved to be worshipped. That is the whole duty and purpose of Man. The Catholic setting is orthodox, and God Almighty doesn't require orthodoxy in terms of worshiping Him. Christians can't just attend church to hear the Mass and receive communion and think all is fine and dandy. Satan, even the Devil, looms large in the midst of the Catholic churches because the priests and the bishops are not rebuking the Devil, so he has no reason to flee. The only reason I stop short from condemning Catholicism is because they believe in Jesus Christ as the son of God. And Jesus Christ is the head of Christianity, not the Pope. Enough said. Thank God for the Pentecostals who are not ashamed to worship God with all their hearts and whose only shepherd is Jesus Christ, even the Son of the Highest.

My ultra-extreme views have led everybody and their uncle to conclude that I am not a Christian. Because I don't speak it but they admit that I live it. That is to say, I walk the walk of a Christian but I don't talk the talk of a Christian. I act like one but I don't talk like one. But many of Christ disciples left Christ after they couldn't continue to stomach the things (the truth) that Christ was speaking about.

Jesus said, "If any man comes to me, and hates not his father, and mother, and wife, and children, and brethren, and sisters, yea, and his own life also, he cannot be my disciple" (Luke 14:26). In the Gospel of John 6:53, 54, 56, Christ said "Verily, verily, I say unto you, Except ye eat the flesh of the Son of Man, and drink his blood, ye have no life in you. Whoso eateth my flesh, and drinketh my blood, hath eternal life; and I will raise him up at the last day. He that eateth my flesh, and drinketh my blood, dwelleth in me, and I in him."

Now after Christ uttered these words, it states in verse 66 "From that time many of his disciples went back, and walked no more with him." And many of those disciples that Christ appointed were chronicled in Luke 10 verses 10 and 17 respectively.

And I have been called a child of the Devil more than I have been called a child of God, solely because I'm against abortion, gay marriage, and freedom without virtue. But Christ was called a devil in many occasion by the Pharisees. If I wasn't a conservative, if I wasn't an adherent of Rush Limbaugh and Sean Hannity, the world would have upheld me as a saint.

My belief in God is an eternal breath. I have all my eggs in one basket because my belief in God is not shared nor compromised; I have an unshakable belief in God.

Fornication

The moral and biblical principle of being a virgin before marriage has gone the way of the dinosaur. Who is to the right of Jesus Christ? True conservatives begin their preaching against abortion; I begin my preaching against fornication—the very act itself. Jesus the Savior of Man began His preaching on the intent on lusting.

What predates abortion? What comes before abortion? So if I should begin my critique on abortion from abortion in itself, it means that I'm wrong. So I begin my critique from the act of fornication. The average conservative begins their critique from abortion in itself. But I begin my critique from sex before marriage. But Jesus Christ began his critique from the thought of lusting after a woman. Should there even be an abortion that occurs between married couples?

In closing, I don't hate any liberals, communists, totalitarians, statists, etc. But I certainly hate their ideology. Their ideology originates from the depths of Hell.

I have the utmost love for ultra conservatives—namely, Tom DeLay, Mark Levin, Rick Santorum, etc. Because it's very easy to profess to be a Christian but it is challenging to admit to being a conservative. Those who claim to be conservative are ready for the challenge. Obama called himself a Christian yet he endorsed abortion and gay marriage. By definition, a conservative who upholds gay marriage and abortion is not a conservative.

Blood is no longer thicker than water. When Jesus was informed that His mother and brethren were waiting afar off to minister to Him, He responded that those who believed in Him are His brethren and His mother. I love my chosen ones (family and friends), albeit the majority of them are liberals. And it's inevitable that we won't sing from the same hymnal. Some of them are liberal in ignorance. If I have liberal friends, they are of yesteryear.

There is no wisdom and there is absolutely no common sense in gay marriage.

Homosexual love is love from the Devil and there are no ifs, ands, or buts about that.

An act of abortion that has been committed is "Thou shall not kill," it's nothing but murder. And each and every one of the culprits is in danger of the Lake of Fire.

I'm a conservative ideologist and I have written books promoting conservatism because in this earthly world, conservatism is the cutting edge ideology. My God-given wisdom has made me know everything pertaining to conservatism. Christ is the pinnacle of Christianity.

Chapter 3

Perfected Worship

———⌇∽⊸⊶⊷⊶⊸∽⌇———

Jesus's Ultimate Sacrifice

How many hours did Christ spend in the grave below? Jesus was in the grave for nine hours on Friday; twenty-four hours on Saturday and seven hours on Sunday, which is the first day of the week—for a total of approximately forty hours that Jesus the Savior was in the sepulcher for Man. Imagine and envisage the Son of God in the grave below for the sinners of the world.

Christ gave up the ghost at the ninth hour on Friday. And on the ninth hour on Saturday He was in the sepulcher. But before the ninth hour on Sunday befell, Christ had risen to Heaven. So in essence, Christ only spent one ninth hour (which was on Saturday) in the tomb. In the first ninth hour, Christ died for mankind on the cross of Calvary. In the second ninth hour, Christ was resurrected for mankind, and in the third ninth hour, Christ was already interceding for mankind in Heaven.

Christ died on the sixth day of the week, which was on a Friday, which was the sixth day that God created Man; hence, Christ died for the sins of Man. Christ died on the sixth day, which is also the number of Man, because Man was created on the sixth day of creation and it's appointed for Man to die; hence, Christ being the son of Man died on the sixth day. On the seventh day which was on Saturday, God rested, as His creation was finished. And Christ, after he uttered "It is finished," gave up the ghost. And Christ was in the grave below and rested on the seventh day. Throughout the seventh day Christ was in the grave below. Christ was in the grave for twenty-four hours. It was the only day that Christ was in the grave for a whole day. On the first day of the week, which was on Sunday, Christ resurrected from the dead and ascended to Heaven. On the first day of creation is when God the Father, the Son, and the Holy Spirit created the Heavens and the earth.

You own your sins—lock, stock, and barrel. And if you die in your sin, your own blood will be upon your head. Should you take the life of a person, the blood of that innocent person will be on your head. And just as the blood of Abel cried out to God after Cain slayed Abel, the blood of that person will wail out to God and you will be hunted. You will be passed unto judgment if someone's blood is upon your head.

Jesus was the culprit for the sins of mankind so His death wasn't in vain.

Earth was cursed and earth became sin. When Christ died, Christ took our sins and buried them in the grave. And rather than Christ becoming dust, our sins became dust. So it wasn't Christ that was buried when He died, it was the sins of all human beings that was buried. In other words, Christ bore our sins to the grave; hence, when we pass away, Christ will resurrect those who believe in Him on the last day.

If you suppose that you are doing God a favor by attending the tabernacle and by worshiping Him, then you have another think coming. Christ did Man an eternal favor by dying for the sins of Man. We should live by God's favor. Man's favor is vanity.

"For God so loved the world that He sent His only begotten son." Jesus gave His life as a ransom for the sins of the world, for the sins of mankind. We will never fathom how much it cost Christ to die for us.

Christ went to the grave below for us so we would be saved from the second death. Christ's death was an eternal victory for mankind over sin. Christ didn't need a victory for Himself because the whole world is in His hands; all powers, even the powers of Satan, are under Christ's feet.

Remember that the ninth hour was the hour that Christ died. Time is of the essence. Jesus warns us to be wise as serpents. Any wise enemy of yours is wiser than an ignorant friend of yours. There is time for everything. There is time to be comradelier with your ignorant friends and there should also be time to learn wisdom from God. And

God will put the Devil out there to teach you a lesson. But what do you learn from the lesson? It's easier to be wiser after the events.

Be appreciative of the time, for God does everything just right on time. The cream will surely rise to the top. Christ appreciated the time, although He chomped at the bit for the cup to pass from Him when it was almost time to be crucified. Ecclesiastes chapter 3 states that there is time for everything under the sun. Don't question the time. Don't question whether it's time to work or whether it's time to slumber. Rather, question your actions and deeds within the time; question your utterances and sermons within the time. Are they righteous or evil?

I don't have the time to hate or to be jealous and envious of people. God has not given me that time. God has given me the time to worship Him. God has not given me the time to fornicate, idolize, or blaspheme. God will question you on what you did with the time He afforded you with while on earth.

Tools Against God

It goes without saying that God is worthy. If you are not worshiping God, then you are conniving with the devil; you have extended an olive branch to the Devil. If you are not worshiping God, you have rebelled against and run afoul of God's Word; you are in league with the Devil and become a full-fledged emissary of the Devil. Haven't we seen this movie before? Isn't it everywhere in the Bible? And what was the fate of those who blaspheme the Word of God?

My main goal in life is to draw people into the kingdom of God. So if I should call people for conversation and they respond by saying that they are doing God's business as in praying or worshiping God, then I will immediately cease my contact with them. And I would ask for God's forgiveness. The last thing I want to do in this life is to hinder, distract, or interrupt people who were in the process of worshiping God, even if they were dishonest. As long as they claimed to be doing God's bidding my hands are clean.

I won't be an arsenal for Satan to use to distract people from doing the business of God. In other words, I'm not going to be the one to attempt to prevent Christ from dying for us, the sinners of the world, just as the Apostle Peter was. I have just committed another iniquity against God if I stop to think that peradventure they were lying to me because they didn't want my company.

The shoe is on the other foot sometimes when I'm worshipping God; anyone who interrupts me or attempts to interrupt me is an enemy. Even if the culprit is my best friend, she would still be an enemy at that given moment—even if the culprit disturbed me without intending to. I ignore those who try to obstruct me when I'm worshipping God. I have a "Let the dead bury their dead," mindset. Every earthly event at that moment will cease. If I get a call when I'm preparing for or while in the process of worshiping God, my heart says "Let the dead bury their dead."

Devotion

The Spirit of God Almighty can never depart from me because I reverence, pray, and acknowledge the Lord without ceasing, even three times in an hour. So if I'm on the verge of forgetting, He will remind me.

I live a reclusive lifestyle because I loathe when I can't intimately call on God when I want to. I hate being outside my comfort zone. The day I stop worshiping God will never rear its ugly head. I worship God Almighty alone. In my prayers to God Almighty, I bid Him saying, "I don't worship sin. If I worship sin that means that I worship Man and that also means that I worship my helpmeet."

Sin can't pardon my sins. If God only can forgive my sins, then it wouldn't make sense to worship sin. I relate to God that I will not exercise myself before Him every day if I were not worshiping Him. I won't waste time doing so. I worship God daily because I want to give God the reason to repent from saying He regretted creating Man in the first place.

It's incumbent for me to praise the mighty name of God with songs daily. Hence I put a punishment on myself if I'm guilty of dereliction of duty. In order for me to avoid making a rod on my own back, I must tow the line of my own making. I'm ready to self-destruct worshiping God Almighty. I never want the cup to pass from me when I'm worshiping God because I am always in seventh heaven when I worship the Lord.

One way you can experience Heaven here on earth is by worshiping God Almighty in spirit and in truth with praise songs. I sing to God every day of my life. I'm that Gentile, that stone which the Lord said He will raise to worship His name. And I wouldn't give God a reason to regret raising the Gentiles to worship Him. I have to do the things that millions of people unwillingly refuse to do.

Devote and dedicate sincerely everything you do for God Almighty. Although devoting is in the thought of the beholder, God knows the heart. The sand is running out of the hourglass and that is why we have to surrender everything to God Almighty. I pray to God every hour of the day that I am awake and it seems so normal as the years have gone by. I'm a sinner who endeavors hard to live a sinless life every hour of the day that I'm awake. Yet I must confess my iniquity to God every hour that He reminds me. Yet I proclaim to God that I'm the most sinful person in the world. I pray to and acknowledge the Godhead at least three times in an hour and I worship Him with songs in the eventide, morning, and night—in New York time and in London time.

We should worship God in season and out of season; within and without; in private and in public. Worshiping God is the whole duty of Man. Enough said. Jeremiah 2:5 says, "Thus saith the LORD, What iniquity have your fathers found in me, that they are gone far from me, and have walked after vanity, and are become vain?"

What sin has Man found in God? If Man yield not to be worshipful of God, that means that Man has found iniquity in God; God forbid. We should find time to worship God between the early hours of the morning to the late evening of the same day. And this should be done every blessed day; even if it's for five minutes.

If worshiping God doesn't seem like a full-time job, then you have your work cut out for you. Your mind will distract you when worshiping God in spirit and in truth, so you have to have full concentration. To be in the spiritual realm and to do the things of the spirit is challenging. It's no mean feat.

Be aware that there are certain songs of praise that the Devil will sing along with you. It doesn't scare him; hence, sing songs that Satan the Devil won't dare sing. "My soul magnifies the Lord, and my Spirit praises His name; for death could not hold Him captive even in the grave Jesus is Lord." That is a song of substance; the song quoted the Virgin Mary in Luke chapter 1 and Satan won't dare sing that song or any song of substance.

There is no limit in worshiping the Lord. Idle time is the Devil's workshop, so substitute idle time with worship time. Too much of everything is bad, but not so for having too much of the things of God, because we can never praise God enough. There is no limit or boundary to how much prayer and praise from us that God requires. The Word of God, even the Holy Bible, is infinite wisdom.

There is no complacency in the eyes of God. You can't be content with the things of God because we can never be sufficient in our praise to God. You could pray all day long, yet that is not enough in the sight of God. So the time curfew to do the things of God should be done righteously and with a pure heart. We can never rest on our laurels when dealing with God.

I fast the first seven days of every month, which in so doing covers each day of the week. It's no mean feat to deny yourself the comfort and the luxuries of life, but it's not by one's might nor by one's power, but it's the Spirit of God that enables one to perform such acts. My fasting is dry fasting, that is abstinence from food and water. Anything that goes into my mouth must be regurgitated. I fast so often that I have to think twice before I put food in my mouth; just to be sure that I wasn't fasting. Every week day I undergo an unuttered fasting. That is, I don't confess to God that I'm fasting via the mouth, but confess via my heart, because once you confess to God that you're fasting for certain hours, Satan will ready his arsenal and his temptations hover around. But the only way I could undergo an unuttered fasting is by worshiping God throughout the fasting period.

Retaining Love

I told God adamantly that I want to retain all the love He has given me to use to love Him. I don't want to share the love I have for God with the material world. I have the utmost love for God; I'm addicted to worshiping God and studying the Word of God. Those are my only addictions in life. The more you love God, the less you sin. I love the holiness of God as much as I love God Himself.

The Word of God is innate in me. Worshiping God with songs of praise and doing what is right at all times are inherent in me. It just has to be remembered. Sin is also inherent in me because while men slept, sin suppressed the Word of God in me. The Word of God and songs of God keep me on the cutting edge.

Let it be common sense to utter "good morning" to God every morning that we wake from sleep. What is the purpose of life? Give God a reason to keep you alive. Create anticipation with God; tell Him what you will do for Him each passing day. Let the Word of God live rent-free in your head. Man should not live by bread alone but by every word that comes out of the mouth of God. At the beginning of every day, I make it incumbent that reading the Word of God is the first thing I do.

In some part of the world, Christ is fast becoming something of a forgotten Man. The babe leapt for joy while he was in his mother's womb but you no longer leap for joy when you mature into a teenager. You no longer leap for joy when you mature into an adult, but while you were in the womb of your mother, you heard the Gospel and you leapt for joy. You refused to acknowledge God; you put God on the back burner. You intentionally forgot about what made you joyful while in the uterus of your mother. What is in the womb of a mother? Nothing compared to the world in which the babe is born into. The cares of the world has overwhelmed and engulfed you hook, line, and sinker. John the Baptist, while in his mother's womb, leapt for joy when he heard the voice of Mary who was to bear the Son of God. John the Baptist leapt for joy in his mother's womb and when he was born into the world, he leapt for joy because he was honored to be chosen as the forerunner of Jesus Christ. He leapt for the joy of being elected to baptize Jesus Christ, even the son of God. Jonah leapt for joy for the Word of God but he was remanded to the womb, this time in a whale, to recapture the joy of God. God can send you to incarceration and to isolation to remember that first love.

What is your lot for God in this life? As soon as Christ took His last breath, as soon as midnight fell on crucifixion day, man started living on borrowed time. Man was left to his own devices. Thank God Almighty for Jesus' last breath.

If you say God is good then make certain you're speaking from the heart. Don't give lip service to the Almighty God in Heaven, because you're better off not saying anything.

You have to keep all the precepts and commandments of God; the status and ordinances of God must be upheld if you believe that God is good. God is good when Mother Nature and manmade destruction culminates in untold carnage; God is good all the time. When the feet of those who buried your husband are waiting to bury you, God is good. If disaster hits home and none that piss against the wall survive, is God still good? If things are not going as planned, then God has testified against me. But Christ intercedes on my behalf, and the Holy Spirit prays for me too, so there will always be hope on the horizon.

Critics

In my prayer to God, I beseeched my Lord, "I don't want to put words in Your mouth." I don't want to intentionally misinterpret the Word of God in order to suit myself. Should I innocently misinterpret the Word of God, then let it win people to the kingdom of God. Yet again, let my misinterpretation be of ignorance to me. Let me not interpret the Word of God with the knowledge that I'm false.

Apostle Paul in preaching said we have to be everything to all men in order to win them to Jesus. But friendship with the world is enmity with God. It's below my pay grade to be involved with the things of the world.

I play devil's advocate as I examine subliminal possible criticisms of my personal Lord and savior Jesus Christ. My subliminal nature gives me the shrewd ability to inquire of hidden biblical questions about Jesus.

In Mark 10 verse 8, Jesus said, "Why callest thou me good? There is none good but one, that is, God." But of course it is common sense that Jesus Christ is good. Christ said, "Why callest thou me good?" because He didn't want to convey to people that being good will led them to salvation.

Why did God express that He hates Esau and loves Jacob? Hate is in the heart of the beholder, but sin foreruns hate. If you hate it means sin is in you. Sin is not embedded nor within God, so how then can God hate? God's hate connotes love. The love exhausted in God's hate toward Esau is greater than the love exhausted in Man's unconditional love for each other.

Can the book of Songs of Solomon redeem you from hellfire? Can the book of Esther—which has no mention of God—redeem you from the second death? Can Man be saved if the book of Songs of Solomon was the only word of God recorded in the Bible?

God in Three Persons

God in Heaven is in three persons: God the Father, God the Son, and God the Holy Spirit. When God created Heaven and earth it was God the Father that spoke the utterance, and it was God the Son (Jesus) that physically created Heaven and earth, and it was God the Holy Spirit that put life in Heaven and on Earth. When God said let "Us" create Man in Our own image, God was referring to the Father, Jesus, and the Holy Spirit.

In order for God to prove that He truly loved the world, He came and died for the beloved creatures which He created in His own image. God had to come to earth as a newborn baby who grew up to be the Messiah, even the King. So God on earth was Jesus Christ and when Jesus Christ departed, Jesus sent the Holy Spirit. So after the death of Christ, the Holy Spirit became God on earth. And when the Second Coming (Jesus Christ) returns, the Holy Spirit will depart from earth and ascend back to Heaven.

For example, Jacob and Esau were brothers from the loins of Isaac. To his kindred, Jacob was a shepherd by occupation; to his twelve children, Jacob was a father; and to Esau his brother's children, Jacob was an uncle. So Jacob was a father as in God Almighty, Jacob was an uncle as in Jesus Christ, and Jacob was a farmer as in the Holy Spirit. At the end of the day, Jacob is still one person; just as at the end of the day, God Almighty is still one God. God is Father in Heaven and God was Christ on earth, and when Christ rose from the dead to Heaven, God became the Holy Spirit on Earth.

The way, the truth, and the life: Christ is the way, the Holy Spirit is the truth, and the Almighty God is the life. The Way's mission on earth is already finished but not yet completed. The completion will culminate when Satan, that great dragon, is finally defeated. The Truth abides on earth with Man. The Truth is the One who bids and urges Man to do what is right: the right conscience of Man, the still small voice if you will, the first of the two thoughts of Man.

The Life is immensely holy to be on earth. God Almighty sits on His throne in Heaven patiently awaiting judgment of the creatures He created in His own image on the sixth day.

The lifetime of Man on Earth is spent only with the Truth. The Truth teaches us the Way to salvation and that Way is Jesus Christ. The only Way we can regenerate to Heaven is through believing that Jesus Christ is the Son of God. When a Man gives up the ghost, he or she is now faced with the Life. And if you believe in the Way and in the Truth's advice, then you will have Everlasting Life; but if you were heedless to the Truth, rest assured that Satan will have you for company and there will be gnashing of teeth. In the lake of fire, even in the abyss, it will be too late to say "Would to God that I had listened to the Truth while I was still alive on earth."

The way of fornication, the way of theft, and the way of deceit, etc. are all the way to the second death. But the way to Calvary is the only true way; it's the way to salvation. Jesus is the manifestation of the Word of God that was spoken into life. In order words, the Word of God is Jesus that was spoken into life. John 1:1 states that "In the beginning was the Word [Jesus] and the Word [Jesus] was with God, and the Word [Jesus] was God." Hebrews 1: 8-9 also confesses that Jesus was the one who created the world.

There are three degrees to the Word of God: the unadulterated word of God spoken by Christ in the Gospel; the word of God spoken through the prophets, most especially Moses, Isaiah, and Jeremiah; and the word of Man inspired by the Spirit of God, which are the psalms of David, the proverbs of Solomon, etc.

The Saved and the Condemned

God is good and Satan is evil. You can't love God and be a faithful servant to Satan; you can't love God and repudiate His works. You can't have your cake and eat it too. You can't serve God on one hand and serve Satan on the other hand.

You kick against the goads if you run afoul of God's ordinances. If the truth is not in you then you savor to do the things of man, not the things of God. You profess your love for God but in your next breath, you blaspheme and abominate the name of the Lord. You are among the sons of perdition.

If you give alms to the needy and you want it to count as good works, that implies that it doesn't emanate from the heart. You give alms because it's coming from your heart. But the Bible states that all our work will be judged and tried through fire and those that will be redeemed will be redeemed based on what they did on earth. So if we can't be saved by our good works, then why will our works on earth be tested and judged by God?

The soul of every believer will be saved by the grace of God. Although the good works of Christians, Muslims, etc. will be saved, the souls of those who didn't believe in Jesus Christ will not be saved. By and large, believing in Jesus is the only road to salvation; salvation for mankind is by the grace of God. In essence, it's only by the grace of God that Man will be redeemed; it's only by truly believing that Jesus Christ is the Son of God that will save mankind.

Jesus said if you feed the poor, you have fed me; the feeding of the poor is a good work. But the Bible said we can't be saved by our works. So the feeding of the poor that Jesus spoke of must be done with the belief in the person's heart that Jesus is Lord and Savior. The whole bottom line is that good works can't be good works if the philanthropist is not a believer of Christ.

The prejudgment of God has been passed already. Christ said, "For I was hungry and you gave me something to eat, I was thirsty and you gave me something to drink, I was a stranger and you invited me in, I needed clothes and you clothed me, I was sick and you looked after me, I was in prison and you came to visit me" (Matthew 25:35-36). That is the prejudgment Jesus has passed unto Man. If you heed and adhere to the two commandments of God and the prejudgment of Jesus then you will be your own judge; you will judge yourself to Heaven. Then you have remained on good footing to make it to Heaven. Having said that, you must believe that Jesus is the Son of God.

God really, truly loves Man and He will give you ample chances to repent; ample chances to fall on the Stone so as to avoid being ground to powder. God is a merciful God but because of the accuser of the Brethren, there is only so much God can do—even though God can do anything. At the end of the day it is up to you to repent and atone from your wicked ways. Wicked ways are not exclusively doing what is evil; wicked and evil ways are not worshipping God. Recall to your memory Jeremiah 2:19. It's only a wicked son or daughter that doesn't appreciate their father ransoming His life for them.

How hard is it to kick against the goads? If you choose to be stubborn and fail to yield to God's calling, then the road of Damascus will be your fate. God will only summon evil spirits to correct and chastise you and bring you back to repentance. The evil spirit from God is clearly distinguished from the evil spirit from Satan. Paul's road to Damascus was a lifelong lesson. Paul didn't seek a second opportunity to repent from breathing out threats upon the Christians. Paul repented at the first time of asking.

God will only testify against you if He loves you. He longs for you to repent and do His will.

How can you profess that you love God when you don't even know Him? You don't revere Him. You call His name only in passing; you idolize the world. Why do you suffer earth to be your heaven? If the sun refused to smite you by day, the moon will surely smite you by night. If God doesn't punish you on earth, then He will punish you in Hell Fire. You willingly refuse to heed to the Spirit of Truth which is the Holy Spirit, so the feet of those that buried all the atheists, heathens, and unbelievers are waiting yonder to bury you, too, thus making you a statistic. Your ego couldn't let you bring and summit yourself to believe that Jesus is the Son of God, so as the atheists, heathens, and unbelievers were buried, so too were the Rabbis and the Imams waiting to be buried. "Thou shalt worship the Lord thy God," that made the Heaven and the earth, which is the greatest of all commandments; hence the feet of those that buried all the atheists, heathens, and unbelievers are waiting to bury hero worshippers and the idolaters of the world. Give your life to God; take your last breath in your disbelief in God Almighty. If you stubbornly refuse to give your life to God, on that dreadful day the Lord will say, "I know you not ye workers of iniquity."

Give God a reason to give you more than two visits. God only considers you when you were born and when you die. All throughout your life on earth, God never inquires of you because you never beseech Him. You never worship Him with new songs; you never study the Holy Scriptures. You only made mention of God's name in vain. You never made Him to ponder about you. God sent you to the world with a mission but you never ventured on the mission; hence, the Lord only remembers you again when He sends the spirit of death to take you away. And when you assume room temperature, you do so without instruction from Him. Cornelius gave much alms and prayed to God always; hence, at the ninth hour of the day, God dispatched an angel to inform Cornelius that his prayers and alms have come up as a memorial before Him. Cornelius allowed God to give him more than two visits.

Give your life to God Almighty. Do something good for a change. If God really wants you to repent, rest assured that you will receive the buffeting from the Lord. If you give God the reason to live then you shall not be concerned over an untimely death. Give your life to God today; do not put it off till tomorrow. Do not kick the can down the road because tomorrow is not guaranteed for any Man. Put your house in order in every opportunity you have because even a seer doesn't know when the hourglass finally runs out of sand. A soothsayer doesn't know when the thief will come at night.

Being regenerated to Heaven is not a matter of "can," it's a matter of "will." Christ died for man so that every man "can" make it to Heaven only by believing in Him. But the million-dollar question is "will" you make it? Will you believe in Jesus as the Son of God? Will you repent of your iniquity? Will you be born again? The ball is in your court. And you can't blame Adam, because Christ came and showed us the way we ought to live. If you don't believe in Jesus then Jesus will not resurrect you on the last day. You can hold your breath on that saying; you could take that to the bank.

A true minister of God, Pastor Bassey said, "Don't follow the world because the world is coming to an end," follow God because the Word of God is eternal. Apostle Excel, an esteemed man of the cloth, who visited Hell Fire, said the only language in Hell Fire is the language of water.

I don't worship Man; I don't worship sin. I will rebuke and upbraid any of my loved ones for God. I will rebuke myself too. Remember that God saw the end from the beginning. The day I worship a human being that was created will never rear its head. I will always deny and forbid myself, but I will never deny God.

In closing, Christ died for Man at the ninth hour of the day. Every hour of the day on Saturday Christ was in the grave for Man. And on that fateful Saturday that Jesus was in the sepulcher, it was the only ninth hour that He was in the grave.

In season and out of season, in good times and in bad times, let there be no end to worshiping, praising, and thanking God for everything He has done for us.

I'm not a vessel for Man but I am a vessel for God the Father, God the Son, and God the Holy Spirit. I'm only subjected to the Holy

Spirit on earth and Jesus Christ in Heaven who intercedes for me and my missing rib every day of my life.

I love God even more than I love Heaven. I'm gratified and grateful to God for creating me to be God-fearing, and most importantly for creating me to blissfully love to worship Him. I would rather die in Hell Fire than to stop worshiping God, and Satan could quote me like he quoted Psalm 91.

My only addiction in life is worshiping God too much in my eyes. Christ died for me in order for me to be saved. Man has to be grind to powder; Man has to end up in the second death if he wants to change my mind and persuade me from believing in Jesus. Man should not live by bread alone but by every word that comes out of the mouth of God. Jesus is the mouth of God.

Man can't be saved by his work, because a Jew or a Muslim who does perfectly good work but who doesn't believe in Jesus Christ can't be saved. Your generosity and charity can't save you, and to boot they are but vanity. Recall that Jesus said, "Why callest thou me good?" because He didn't want the Pharisee to assume that being good will lead Man to Heaven.

Jesus died and was survived by those who believe in Him. How many was Jesus survived by? And will you be in the number? The ninth hour was the hour that Christ took His last breath.

Living on earth is living a life of amnesty, and at the end of one's life on earth, amnesty might be pardoned in Heaven or punished in Hell Fire, even the bottomless pit.

Man should live by every word and not by certain words that proceed out of the mouth of God. We should labor to know the meaning of every word in the Holy Bible before we take our last breath. God freely gives us the breath. So we should acknowledge God every waking hour.

If you die in your sin, rest assured that you will be passed unto judgment.

Christ died for us so that we will not die the second death; but we have to believe wholeheartedly in Him that He is the Lord and Savior. You have to be cognizant of the ordinances and the testimonies of God, lest you find yourself wanting. Not every cloud has a silver lining; there is no silver lining in eternal condemnation. So give your life to Jesus today.

Chapter 4

Perfected Wisdom

———∽∿⊶⚬⟬⚬⊶⚬⊶∿∾———

Christ had to die in order for Man to be saved; Man will have to end up in a coma if he attempts to be wiser than me. Wisdom is from God on high so if the truth is not in you, you can't be wise. That is why I emphasized that conservatives are the wise men; the wisdom of liberals is not wisdom from God, rather it is wisdom from Lucifer. When God spoke of Lucifer, He revealed that Lucifer was "full of wisdom." So every gift from God to Man has its duplicate. God's wisdom, knowledge, love, etc. all have it duplicates. The duplicates are from Lucifer. The so-called love that exists between a homosexual couple is not love from God, rather it is love from Satan. But the couple is ignorant and blind to perceive that what they called love is nothing but evil disguised as love.

Wisdom of the South

There are only three people who I considerably learn from in this world: Rush Limbaugh, Apostle Excel, and God the Holy Spirit. Apostle Excel is a highly-reputed man of the cloth from New York. Apostle Excel was reported dead on the tenth day of the ninth month of the year 1989. And just when the ambulance was about to take his body to the mortuary, he woke up. On his journey, God took him to Heaven and Hell. God revealed the Word of God through two of His angles to Apostle Excel.

I listen to people to get messages and signs from God. So it's not solely Rush Limbaugh and Apostle Excel that I harken to. The only difference is that I learn substantially from Rush and Apostle Excel. What I mean by "learning" is that they aggravate my mind. I'm a Man of substance. Karl Rove and Charles Krauthammer are said to be really smart American pundits but they don't hold a candle to Rush Limbaugh. Rush is unrivalled.

Outside of Rush Limbaugh and Apostle Mark Excel, every Man to me is either in one of two brackets: dimwits or mediocre. And Rush and Excel are the only two who I substantially learn from. And I'm sufficient, so I'm not looking for another, like John the Baptist was. People outside of Rush and Excel will deliver a good speech, a brilliant sermon, and a clever message, but it was always going wide. It didn't aggravate my mind. It didn't strike a nerve. By and large it was nothing to write home about. In other words, it lightened, it thundered, but it didn't rain.

Now the principles and values of Rush Limbaugh and the Conservative Manifesto, are they not written in "See, I Told You So?"

Now the biblical visions of Apostle Mark Excel, are they not written in "Crisis Management: A Spiritual Approach?"

The closer you are to God, the more wisdom He bestows upon you. The more you explore and know God, the wiser you become. Having an intimate, close relationship with God is trying to live a sinless life. Pure wisdom emanates from God Almighty.

God is real, true, and holy. Real, true, and holy are all under the umbrella of being nigh to God. The more real, true, and holy you are, the more God bestows you with wisdom. You can't certainly ascertain the wisdom of being real, holy, and true until you become it yourself. God will not impart you with the wisdom associated with being any of the aforementioned until you become real, holy, and true.

Naturally, I'm a real and true individual; hence my wisdom is tested by how true and real I am in any given situation. God made me real and true right from the beginning. And I'm honored that the Most High elected me to be real and true.

How true are you in a position? If you start your peaching against abortion from abortion itself rather than starting your preaching against abortion with being against fornication, then the wisdom of sin has overtaken the wisdom of truth in you. And you will be deprived of the wisdom of truth on that front.

The more spiritual, non-earthly and non-material you are, the wiser you become because worldly, mundane, carnal, and secular things of the world distract one's wisdom. The more you worship God in spirit and in truth the wiser you become. A wise Man cannot be carnal, he must be spiritual, because God is spirit. There is a relationship between sin and wisdom. The more you restrain yourself from sinful acts, the more God empowers you with wisdom.

Christ emphasized the relationship between wisdom and sin. Christ didn't preach as someone who has repented from sin. Repentance was Apostle Paul's portion. Before Paul was converted, he habituated to prosecuting Christians. Christ was without sin so Christ couldn't preach from the repentance platform.

Jesus Christ didn't commit any sin, so He didn't ask to be forgiven before He embarked on preaching the Gospel. Jesus brought wisdom to the world; the world didn't know pure wisdom until Christ came. Jesus had all the wisdom in the world because He was without sin. Sin deducts part of someone's wisdom. If you sin, your wisdom will be halved and deducted, because sin has taken half with it. Sin needs your wisdom in order to overtake the pure wisdom God has bestowed upon you. So sin needs you to sin in order to bestow upon you the craft of the old serpent, even the guile of Satan. Jesus wasn't preaching as someone who had sinned and repented. For that reason He was the wisest person in the world. And when Christ ascended to heaven, the wisdom of Christ on earth was transferred to God the Holy Spirit.

The most time God reveals wisdom to me is when I'm singing and praying—by and large when I'm worshiping Him in any way, manner, or form.

God reveals wisdom to me as I worship Him with songs going to and fro and up and down like Lucifer. Hence I always chomp at the bit to turn idle time, which is the Devil's workshop, to worship time so as to acquire wisdom from God.

I beseeched the Lord to grant me wisdom above all other' wisdoms on earth. And New York City has been a happy hunting ground for me to attain that feat. New York is ground zero. It has been a laboratory for acquiring wisdom as well as a laboratory for testing one's wisdom. It's the foremost place in the world where one could assess his or her wisdom.

The Spirit of wisdom is one of the seven spirits of God. The Lord God imparts me with wisdom through anger. When I get angry and piqued, my mind gets aggravated. Satan comes around with temptation almost immediately and the Spirit of wisdom proceeds too. And my wisdom increases. And oftentimes I intentionally get into heated arguments because I know that once I am aggravated and provoked, the genie is out the bottle and wisdom descends upon me.

I attain wisdom when I am angry and furious because I will be forced to think deeply. When I get mad, it exacerbates my mind and it empowers me with more wisdom because I think long and hard. And Satan uses that opportunity to tempt me, and I won't rebuke the Devil because of the wisdom in the process; I don't want the pouring of wisdom at that instance to cease. So I purposely yield to the Devil's tempting, albeit I know my limits. Anger's aggravation and Satan's enticement endows me with wisdom. Satan and the spirit of anger are my friends, only when I desire for them to be. I control our association.

If I refrained myself from fornication, covetousness, or idolizing, etc., then I will certainly and assuredly stake my claim as the wisest person in the world.

I practice what the Ten Commandments preach; hence, I don't commit grave and abominable sins. I abstain myself from the enjoyment of the world because I'm intent for God to give me towering wisdom. The world enjoys what I hate. I'm not material so the pleasure of sin has eluded me.

I haven't given myself to the reprobates of the world; the bottom line and the reason I don't idolize the earthly and secular things of this world is not solely because keeping God's commandments result to eternal life, but it is because I yearn for God to bestow upon me wisdom above any wisdom on earth. A price must be paid for what we long for. I refuse to be second fiddle to Man; I want my God-given wisdom to be streets ahead and hold a candle to no Man's earthly wisdom.

How can I maintain that I'm better than any Man when I am the one that is handicapped with a lost eye? I live every day of my life to acquire wisdom. No Man can see what I can see.

My ignorance is not due to lack of wisdom but to the lack of being informed or aware; if I'm benighted, it will be due to lack of acclimation. I'm all about substance, so ignorance due to being unaware or uninformed is not substantive to me. Sometimes I act ignorantly before Man so as to avert being bothered.

The best thing in this life that is on the same par as worshiping God is to acquire wisdom and understanding. And I thank the Holy

Spirit earnestly for the wisdom He has graced upon me and also for choosing a vessel like me.

My wisdom compels me to pretend when dealing with people. Hence I suppress my wisdom in order to deal with people because there is no reason to exercise my understanding.

Wisdom makes me a snob. People see me as a snob. If I'm a snob it's because I don't want to be judgmental; I try not to judge people but inescapably it's impossible not to judge people because the shrewd wisdom God embedded in me catapults me to the judging of people.

I reiterate that if I am a snob is not because of class, it's because I hate what is ignorant, sheepish, and trivial.

With all the wisdom God has favored unto me, I doubt if I can plead to God for forgiveness and cite ignorance as an excuse. I'm aware of almost every thought that comes to my mind while awake. It is almost impossible for me to commit a sin without mentally knowing that I have sinned; if I did I would be lying to myself.

Human beings are too easy to detect. They could mop the floor with me but there is no challenge awaiting me from a human being that I can't defeat wisdom-wise. It's easy and very predictable; it's child's play. There is absolutely no competition.

Tons of people learn effectively from me but they don't openly admit it because a prophet has no honor in his hometown. So my reputation goes before me on that front. I sharpen people's intellect; I cause people around me to be wise. My wisdom ricochets to people of my ilk and my acquaintances. I, even I, make illiterates to be smart and to think outside the box. Although acquaintances boomerang my wise tactics against me, they are quick to realize that my wise tactics are infinite and know no bound. I really get stunned that even the illiterate get wiser. Because when I open my mouth, I open my mouth with wisdom; I enlighten people around me, and present them with a new way of thinking. But my wisdom is from God that made Heaven and earth.

The best way to live is in ignorance because the wiser you become, the more you perceive the ugly head of sin. Will I want God to make me ignorant and foolish like the world? No, because we can't tell the Potter how to be made, and because the Potter didn't just make me wise, He imparted me with towering wisdom. Ignorance is truly bliss but an invincible wisdom is worth the worries of knowing.

Sin cannot be wiser than righteousness; sin cannot be wiser than truth. Prostituting cannot be wiser than abstinence. I'm wiser than sin in itself. I'm wiser than any womanizer, drunkard, smoker, etc. I heed to the advice from the Holy Spirit by refusing to let the earthly spirits overtake me.

Wisdom to the North

The Holy Spirit I know, Apostle Excel and Rush Limbaugh I know, but who are you?

It's one thing to believe not in my proclamation of being the wisest person on earth, but it is another thing entirely to issue a challenge. You will have another thing coming and I will let you know all about it. I will let you have it, hence you wouldn't hear the end of it. Rome wasn't built in a day. I didn't wake up one morning, full of wisdom. It took a while; it took burning the midnight oil; it took self-sacrifice and it took abstinence.

So woe unto any Man on earth that is not content with what he knows. You will rue the day you confront to challenge me. There is no doubt that you will be taken to the cleaners. You stepped up and met your nakedness like the sons of Sceva—disgrace and full of regrets with tail behind your back. You enjoyed kicking me while I was down, while the Holy Spirit was readying me for an invincible wisdom. But now I know all the ways of Man and I wouldn't grant you a second invitation.

You'd better be content with what you know lest I will let you have all of it. And that is a warning to all of mankind, even those who don't have honor for a prophet because they are from the same neck of the woods. With all the wisdom God has given me, it will be a joke and an insult for any Man to stand up and challenge me. God has given me the wisdom above any wisdom on earth so as to know all the ways of Man. Woe unto that ingrate that attempts to outsmart my intelligence; woe unto that Man who impugns my God-given wisdom. Don't worry about living to fight another day, because it wouldn't happen.

God has made me to easily and swiftly know all the ways of Man. As a mortal, I want to fathom all the wisdom that is to be revealed in this world by God. I have the capacity. Because I know all the ways of Man, I don't give people the benefit of the doubt without repercussion. Because I know all the ways of Man, I'm never surprised at anything Man does. It was expected; I observed it, so I expected it.

Man is always looking for openings to verbally attack me, but my arsenals of my wisdom are infinite. The moment I start having a conversation with somebody, I have already perceived the end of the conversation. Jesus said take no thought of what you are going to say because the Comforter will equipped you with what to utter. And being that I am a servant of the Holy Spirit, I'm never void of utterance. Because I am consumed by the Holy Spirit, almost every word that came out of the mouth of God is on the tip of my tongue and ready to be uttered. So I can never be vacant when being questioned. But remember that when Christ was interrogated by the Pharisee concerning who gave Him authority, Christ didn't answer their tempting question. So not all the questions that Man queries to you should be answered. Many times I'm forced to answer a question with a question because I have anticipated Man's thought. You have to know the premise of the question being asked. You have to know the devil in the details of one's questioning.

My wisdom of yesterday swiftly becomes stale wisdom for me because I'm always seeking, cajoling, and chomping at the bit for more wisdom from God. I live my life eager and willing to acquire wisdom. Wisdom from God is my all and all—my be-all and end-all. I can't even keep up with the wisdom God has given me. And peradventure that is why God made me love my missing rib so much because her name means wisdom.

I summoned God and during one of my scheduled prayers to God, I deceived the Devil because he distracted me in my prayers and worshiping. I told God that I was only going to worship Him for few minutes but God knew that I was going to worship Him for hours.

My strategy in life is to take an action or an utterance and define it to its last details. What is the cutting edge of wisdom on any given issue? That is where my knowledge begins. And where my knowledge ends is where the Word of God begins. I keep my wisdom on the cutting edge.

For any question I'm being asked, I start at the extreme, at the cutting edge, with what Jesus would respond in answering the question. What Jesus Christ did or what Jesus Christ said, that is where the wisdom of any given issue on earth ends.

I study myself and I try to be attentive and aware of every thought that comes to my mind, albeit it is burdensome to keep track. I try to be aware of the time that passes me by.

Time is precious in terms of staying wise. I have a "get in and get out" mentality. No time to take prisoners, no time for gossip, no time for idle talk, no time to be corrupt, no time to cajole, no time for prostituting, by and large no time to rub shoulders with.

Be alert to what you are being called by people. If people call me a fool and I don't rebuke them, then I have accepted the premise. If people call me a fool and they don't apologize and then I don't rebuff them, that means I have accepted that I am a fool.

When I am confronted with an issue or a situation of my personal concern or of people's concern, I first ponder the degree of seriousness. I start pondering from the end—i.e., the worst possible outcome of such serious condition. And if it's not a matter of life and death or a horrible ruination of character, then I cease from pondering and pronounce my empathy for the person's idle tale. Because to me if it's not a matter of life and death or a grave situation, then all other issues and situations are idle tales.

Your wisdom will let you overlook the offense that people do to you. But the affront of a loved one will hit you close to home and will hit you where it hurts. Although it will be utterly difficult to sneeze at your loved one's offense toward you, remember that a prophet is without honor in his hometown. And the curse that Christ uttered to mankind will last forever. So no Man can ever be totally respected in his hometown or by his own people. Any Man that reckons he has honor in his hometown has called Jesus a liar.

Wisdom to the West

The wisdom of Lucifer is the wisdom that God blessed him with from the beginning, and since Lucifer fell out of God's grace, God ceased from giving Lucifer more wisdom and understanding. Thus, Lucifer's wisdom became stale, which later became crafty. The craftiness of Lucifer first reared its ugly head when the Old Serpent tricked Eve in the Garden of Eden. The first thought of man is from God and is pure wisdom. The second thought of man is crafty, which is also the stale wisdom of Satan.

Solomon was wise but was given a reprobate mind when he worshiped the idols of certain of his hundreds of wives and concubines. And as such, the wisdom of idolatry—hook, line, and sinker—overtook him in his old age. The wisdom of idolatry defiled and rendered Solomon's wisdom of truth useless.

How do you expect to see the end when you didn't see the beginning? How do you expect to harvest when you didn't plant? How do you expect to reap when you didn't sow?

Lucifer wasn't there from the beginning of time yet he desired to see the end of time; he yearned to be like God, and as such he was cast down to earth. Why would you expect a favorable result when there was no blood, sweat, and tears to account for? How do you expect to know the end when you weren't there from the beginning?

God has not appeared to me as He appeared to Apostle Excel on numerous occasions, so I have a reason to doubt His existence, unlike Excel who has no reason to doubt His existence because He appeared to Excel even as He appeared to Moses. But because God has endowed me with towering wisdom, then I will never doubt His existence but make use of the wisdom of God. Solomon was deemed the wisest person on earth before the coming of Christ. But Solomon with all his wisdom worshiped idols. So if Solomon was truly wise, why then did he adulate man-made idols? It begs the question. He turned his wisdom to foolishness. But I wouldn't dare worship idols because I'm fully aware that my existence in this world is by God only. So how wise was Solomon? I maintain to you that Solomon's wisdom ended as soon as he began to worship idols. It's not as if Solomon was a vagabond who came from out of the woods; Solomon was the son of King David and David never once worshiped or knew any idols. The beginning of Solomon's wisdom is the wisdom of truth, but the end of Solomon's wisdom is the wisdom of idolatry, even the wisdom of sin. Solomon was wise but he lacked understanding. Solomon is not a forerunner of my wisdom because I wouldn't end up worshiping idols. Solomon's wisdom doesn't eclipse mine.

My wisdom is beyond human nature; I know all the ways of Man. And as such I have seen the end of Man's wisdom. I have seen the end of common sense on earth. The mentality of all the people that I have encountered, come across, and associated with in Europe, Africa, and America is just solid evidence. Almost everything people say or do, I anticipate. Nothing people do surprises me; nothing people do is not expected. It might tarry but there is only so much delay it could tolerate. Nothing people do or say passes me by without me perceiving it.

My wisdom is given freely from God. My wisdom is common sense; my wisdom has made me the most perceivable and the shrewdest. I'm not better than any human being in this world but obviously I'm wiser than—and "wiser than" is an understatement. I mean, I have seen the end of Man's wisdom; I know all the ways of Man. Man's wisdom ends where mine begins.

You can only involve yourself in things within the range of your wisdom. Hence, I don't condemn those who participate in the pleasures of the world and those who chomp at the bit to have good times, because that is where their wisdom ends. It's not immoral or ungodly to enjoy the pleasures of the world, but certain ones have been earmarked against such, and I happen to be one who has been reserved. I steadfastly refuse to tow the line of the world.

People wonder why I'm so earnestly gracious and cordial to people. If I were not respectful, polite, and courteous to people, that means that I am competing with Man. I am naturally a charismatic person and I wouldn't feel comfortable if I didn't greet people along my way because there is no one out there who I'm competing with. Nobody knows what I know so all I could do is to feel guilty and say "good morning" whether to older or younger acquaintances, because Man generally wants warmth and pleasure; that is all they need, so I give them what they crave. But all I long for is wisdom from God. Isn't it common sense that everybody wants to be in authority; everybody wants to call the shots? So I called all fellow colleagues along my way "boss." Give them all the titles in the world and they will never be satisfied. But yet again, all I need is wisdom from God.

When I sincerely greet people, I'm also pitying them; I'm also dismissing them in a way. It's the height of killing two birds with one stone because I view them as children. So by and large, my kindness toward Man is throwing them a bone. That is why I can't get in a fight or in a substantial argument with people because I am never competing with Man; Man has nothing on me.

Without second thoughts, I apologize freely to people if I am wrong in the slightest because of the invincible wisdom God has bestowed upon me. No one knows what I know so why shouldn't I apologize? If I were just the average Joe, it would take till the cows come home before I utter an apology. Everyone to me is a little child; and do you learn from children? Yes, perhaps, but nothing worthwhile. I have to live a pretentious life in order to live this life.

If you are asked to do something or if you are asked for a favor, and you display an antagonizing attitude, then that recalcitrant attitude you displayed has exposed the end of your knowledge. If someone hurls a curse word at you and you curse that person back, you have exposed the end of your knowledge. If someone slaps you and you slap the fellow back, then that is the end of your knowledge. So in essence, the knowledge of "an eye for an eye" ends where the knowledge of "turning the other cheek" begins.

If you support abortion then the end of your knowledge has been exposed. But if you are against abortion then your knowledge never ends. The same goes for homosexual marriage, etc. If you stand against the Gospel then your knowledge has ended. If you are against the truth then your knowledge has ended. If you are against fornication then your knowledge has not ended, but if you condone the act of fornication, etc., then your knowledge has come to an end. As long as your opinion is the opinion of the Word of God, then your knowledge never comes to an end.

Don't let your knowledge end. Don't let Man's issues bring your knowledge to an end.

If you have animosity toward people, then that is the end of your wisdom. If you hold grudges against people, then rest assured that is the end of your wisdom. If you are envious, jealous, or malicious toward people, then that is the end of your wisdom.

If you killed one bird with one stone in any of your endeavors, then that is the end of your wisdom. If your face betrays anger or annoyance when you are being asked for help, then your wisdom has ended. If you are not colorblind, then you have subjected yourself to prejudice, bigotry, and stereotyping; hence, your wisdom has ended. If you happen to find yourself in idle time and you don't swiftly fill that vacuum, then the end of your wisdom has come upon you. If you don't believe that Jesus Christ is God Himself, then that is where your wisdom ends. The end of one's wisdom is when you give someone an attitude because you are asked to do something.

Wisdom to the East

My wisdom is to the East. No human being can ever see the end of my wisdom and understanding. The root of my wisdom stems from the Word of God; hence the end of my wisdom is the beginning of the Word of God.

My God-given wisdom can't contend with this place called Earth; there is nothing to learn from Man except the Word of God; hence, Apostle Excel is my mentor. The Holy Spirit is my mentor, but why am I itched that Rush Limbaugh is the wisest person on earth? Rush never ceases to amazed me.

A wise Man must be known. You must have a bully pulpit; you can't be wise for yourself. A wise person cannot be ignorant. A wise person must be colorblind if he or she abides in a racial society. The wisest person in this world can never be a liberal or of other related ideology. The wisest person in this world must be a conservative. Because the liberal premise is embedded in lies and dribble, and wisdom is the unadulterated truth. Liberals, regardless of how smart they are, can't be wise because they deprive themselves of the truth. If you deprive yourself of the truth, then you are, for all intents and purposes, witless. You might be smart among fellow liberals, but in reality and in the truth, you are one of the fools sitting at the gate idle.

The wisest person on earth can't be wise if he or she supports abortion, gay marriage, freedom without virtue, etc. There is no wisdom in homosexual marriage. Homosexual marriage is an issue that only fools believe in. And if you believe in, uphold, and condone homosexual marriage, then your elevator doesn't reach the top floor. If you support abortion, then you are a few fries short of a Happy Meal. If you think freedom should come without judgment, then you are far from being the sharpest knife in the drawer. If you believe in the notion of equality, then I refer you to one of Christ's parables in Matthew chapter twenty. If you support any of these aforementioned issues, then you have deprived yourself of the wisdom associated with the given issues; by and large you are hoodwinked. I kid you not.

In a particular generation on earth, King Solomon was the wisest man in the world; God confessed to Solomon's wisdom and gave him the bully pulpit of a king, even the king of Israel. Jesus Christ was and will forever be the wisest Man in this world and His Father gave Him a bully pulpit of a Savior. Under the tutelage of Christ, Rush Limbaugh by surrogating is the wisest person in the world; God has given Rush the bully pulpit of a truth detector. Rush Limbaugh's program has the largest audience in the whole wide world with over thirty million audience listeners. That statistic (thirty million) speaks volumes; that statistic is irrefutable and undeniable evidence and a true measure of who the wisest person in the world is. To boot, for more than a quarter of a century, Rush Limbaugh has been at the pinnacle, maintaining the largest audience in the world.

Rush Limbaugh often affirms that he is "a talent on loan from God," not a talent on loan from Man. Rush acknowledges time and time again that his wisdom emanates from God. The day Rush Limbaugh passes away will be the end of America; Rush is the wisest person in this world bar none, and I'm saying this as someone who knows all the ways of Man. When Rush Limbaugh regularly remarks, "half of his brain tied behind his back," he is not pulling anyone's legs.

What will I do without the wisdom that God has bestowed upon me? Isn't that what gives me life? And what is this to me that God has chosen a vessel like me to impart an invincible wisdom? I see countless people devoid of wisdom and understanding. And what would I do if God didn't choose a vessel like me to impart wisdom? Every day I witness people who are void of wisdom and void of the riches of the world and it dampens me, but can I sympathize with them? Wouldn't that be questioning my Maker? So all I can do is worship the Potter rather than questioning why the work of His hands seems or is judged to be witless.

My wisdom is the greatest intangible gift that God has ever blessed me with. My throne is above any other Man's throne on earth. And I tell you truly that it wasn't only Jesus' shoe lace that John the Baptist wasn't fit to tie. No Man's throne is above my throne; my throne is built by the Holy Spirit Himself every given day with the wisdom He instills on me freely.

I'm I embedded with wisdom because of all the life experiences I have been through? It seems as though the wisdom has been there from birth, just waiting to be remembered. It seems I was innate with wisdom because the wisdom of the world seems to be something I knew already, and that I just had to be recalled by the working of the Holy Spirit.

The Holy Spirit gave me the spirit and the wisdom of colorblindness. My parents are Nigerian and I spent seventeen years in Nigeria without growing up with Caucasians. As a kid growing up, I was taught to never hate Whites, so coming back to America, I would have done a three-sixty if I just from left field started abhorring White people because of society's false perspective. Conservatism is the cutting edge and the foremost wisdom on earth. The Holy Spirit deployed Rush Limbaugh to teach me the wisdom of conservatism and deployed Apostle Excel to reveal and to teach me the wisdom of the Word of God. The wisdom of the Word of God is the wisdom of eternal life. I took it from there and I didn't need a second invitation. So I owe Rush Limbaugh and Apostle Excel a debt of gratitude that can be paid in the long run, but I owe the Holy Spirit a debt of gratitude that can never be paid. So my earthly wisdom is sufficient. Hence, I have seen the end of earthly wisdom.

If you start from top, the only way is down. I didn't start from top; I worked my way to the top with the help of boot camp experiences: New York City life experiences, and the wisdom of Steven Howse, Bryon McCane, Anthony Henderson, Rush Limbaugh, Apostle Excel, and of course God the Holy Spirit, has been there for me from the beginning, even from the foundation. The Holy Spirit has been guiding, lecturing, and imparting me with wisdom from the Word of God and now my throne is above every other Man's throne.

God has perfected the wisdom He has given to me. And what is perfect can't be devalued, it can only be added unto. Lucifer was made perfect in beauty but not in wisdom. If Lucifer was made perfect in wisdom he wouldn't have attempted to build his throne above the throne of God; he wouldn't have rebelled against God.

I sense the pinnacle of wisdom when I really get serious in life. Satan took Christ to the pinnacle of the temple and showed Christ the beautiful world. I have reached the pinnacle of wisdom, but unlike Christ, everything that follows me is anticlimactic. The pinnacle of wisdom means I go back to the worldly life, but I wouldn't turn my back from God, unlike Solomon. And I confess to you that having the utmost wisdom from God and knowing all the ways of Man is nothing short of ecstasy and joy.

The wisdom that God has given me is second to none; a wisdom that is bar none from the wisdom of Man and from the wisdom of sin. It's above every other wisdom under God's footstool. God has empowered me with wisdom, knowledge, and understanding to know Man. I know all the ways of Man. I'm in a league of my own.

In closing I say if God didn't destine me to be wise He wouldn't have given Iifi as my missing rib and He wouldn't have put Rush and Excel in my path. Rather, He would have deserted me in Nigeria to be amongst the crowd—a local lad, if you will.

The meaning of my missing rib's name is wisdom. My wisdom comes from God the Holy Spirit. I tell you the truth that if there is someone on the face of the earth that is wiser than me, Ndyfreke Nenty, then I have failed. I mean Jesus Christ had to die in order for my sins to be forgiven. So any person in this world who is wiser than I in this life will end up in a vegetative state for the rest of his life. At age 33, Rush Limbaugh, Apostle Excel, and the Holy Spirit are the only people that I learn from and I listen religiously to them.

I have long seen the end of human nature. If you are a jack of all trades, you will never be a master of one; everything would look like nails because all you have is a hammer. And what is this to me that God should choose a vessel like me to impart an unconquerable, enviable, unattainable, towering, and an insurmountable wisdom? Wisdom is my territory; hence, I am not going to build on another person's foundation. My wisdom is progressive. Anyone can "drink of the cup that I drink of" and can mop the floor with me, but wisdom is my territory. This point in my life is about critiquing but not criticizing the Word of God, because to me that is the only knowledge left to ascertain on earth. For instance, take the temptation of Jesus by Satan. I want to acquire all the wisdom in the Word of God; I want to define it to the lowest possible definition. I'm all about the pinnacle, the foremost, and the greatest.

I love wisdom as much as I love worshiping God Almighty with praise songs and hymns; wisdom is the Holy Spirit that abides within me. God didn't concur with me while He formed me that I would be second fiddle to Man in terms of wisdom. So the wisdom of Man will always be behind me. To me it is all about the pinnacle. Because I have reached the pinnacle of wisdom, I have seen the end of wisdom on earth, which is the end of wisdom to the West. It would take God not being God, for someone to be wiser than me. There is no conceivable way for someone to be wiser than me unless I'm not worshipping God. The end of Man's wisdom has come before me. Any Man that claims to be wiser than me is like Lucifer trying to be like God, like Lucifer trying to build his throne above the throne of God Almighty. This just in, the name "Nndy," means unadulterated wisdom. The only thing that I'm learning to know in this life on earth is the Gospel of God, which is the wisdom to the East; it's a continuous learning curve.

I live my life being observant of what is not occurring.

Chapter 5

Man's Ignorance

————〜〜ᴏᴇ﹩ᴏ·ᴏᴇᴏ﹩ᴏᴡᴍ————

The Potter and the Clay

You live a topsy-turvy life; your life is at sea because you refuse to let the truth abide with you. You become undeterred with the call for repentance. You are desirous for God to deliver you from illness but when did you sow the seeds of worshipping, praise, charity, and tithes to God? Because all else has failed, you now turn to God; hence you call on God in desperation. Don't desperate times call for desperate measures?

When your best years were present before you, when your best years were ahead of you, you didn't call on God. You chose to put God on the back burner. You worked your socks off in season and out of season until your best years were behind you. Your best years are gone and you now yearn to give God your all. But God is not mocked.

I will bring out the long knives for men who ignore God Almighty. I will be chomping at the bit to condemn those men who blaspheme against the Lord. The evil in me is to see the fall of men who steadfastly refuse to acknowledge and glorify God. We have ample time to read and study the Holy book of God and know about God, but we refuse to comply. Whereas the holiness of God wouldn't judge those who are ignorant. If God made me a judge, almost the whole world would be condemned to the deepest depth of Hell. I'm a sinner, so I'm biased; hence I will spare true conservatives and die-hard Christians. I want the worship of God to be mandatory law, and for anyone who refuses to comply, there will be repercussions, ramifications, and penalties.

Why should I sympathize for strangers who died? Who died and made me God? Why should I even think twice about the heathen and the unbelievers who perish? Who died and made me a Potter or a Creator? How can you accuse me of seeing the end from the beginning? How can you equate me with God? How can you calumniate me of trying to build my throne above the throne of the Almighty? I'm only but clay, and clay doesn't give life. It's only the Potter who gives life, so blame the Potter for the carnage.

Why should I lose sleep about the collateral damage that goes on in the world? Why should I worry a bit about people dying all over the world due to wars in Africa, Asia, etc. I didn't know that I'm the Almighty God who created Man. I didn't know that I created the world in six days. I didn't know that the whole world is in my hands? I thought that it's appointed that Man must die? So if I'm not God then why should I lose sleep about people who are dead or in poverty or in distress? I thought I had a younger brother who died when I was under the tutelage of my father growing up in Nigeria. Where is the mourning and the lamentation from the world for my late brother?

It's a small matter for people to die but is a big deal if the deceased didn't give his or her life to Jesus Christ. The Son of God dying for Man wasn't in vain. Nsemeke, my brother, died two years after birth, so if you fall, then you fell; if you die, then you died. Let the dead bury their dead.

A Christian will not die like a chicken. The wars in Africa, Asia, etc. are part of mankind; they are part of life. My brother gave up the ghost, so I have a sense of death. Nobody wants to talk about death, nobody wants to die—except perhaps those in a vegetative state, or on life support, or even those in a coma. But a time will come during Armageddon that Man will be desirous to die but the spirit of death will depart earth. And to make matters worse, God the Holy Spirit will no longer be on earth. Woe unto any Man who will be born in those days. In those days the Antichrist will rule the world and the elite in Christ will be persecuted day in and day out until, if they don't continue to persevere, the mark 666 will be written on their forehead. And they would to God they were not born in those days where the spirit of death was on the horizon. The time will come that Man will be praying to die rather than praying to live.

Lucifer, Cain, Esau, Ishmael, and Judas Iscariot—can they question God for making them? Can they question the Potter? They were all destined by God. Would it have been better if they were not born? You have to pray to be on God's good side; you just have to adhere to God's commandments and precepts.

Human Nature

Don't promise to do something for someone and at the end of the day, sneeze at what you promised. Man is governed by his lip service; it's very easy to utter a promise but it's hard to carry out the promise. You offer lip service just to get praise, but when it's time to deliver, you look the other way with an angry demeanor. If you reneged on a promise, it doesn't mean that you owe a debt. Promising doesn't mean you owe, but don't promise without carrying out your vow, lest you dishearten the heart of the fellow. Don't put your foot in your mouth. Let it be God only that will prevent you from fulfilling that promise.

You do something intolerable to an acquaintance because you previse that at the end of the day you will apologize. "Sorry," of course you are sorry, what else will you say? What were you expecting to say apart from sorry? How can you be apologetic when you knew beforehand exactly what you were doing, and when you knew beforehand that all you have to utter is "sorry" to the victim?

The victims shouldn't accept the premise of an apology lest they will be lying to themselves. You made a fool of yourself to say you are sorry when you were aware of exactly what you were doing. And if the victim accepts that you are really sorry, then the victim has made a fool of himself or herself. The victim has been deceived hook, line, and sinker.

How apologetic are you? That is how we sin against God because we know that at the end of the day, God is a forgiving God. You can offer lip service to Man with all sorts of cajoling and flattering apologies, but you can't offer lip service to God. God knows the heart.

Everybody wants to be some type of foreman. So in the job market, I call everyone along my way "boss." Many accept my polite reverence, while few object. To those who object I know that they eventually want to be a shepherd to flocks; and once they get to the seat of power—catbird seat, if you will—their attitude changes instantly, even without their countenance changing. That is the nature of Man. Give Man an inch and he eventually wants a yard.

A prophet has no honor in his hometown; you could gainsay all day that you do have honor for a known prophet along your way, but it's human nature to deny the notion. So in order to prevent people from lying to themselves, I let them know from the onset that they don't have any honor for me.

I'm known by those in my neck of the woods but they are faceless to me; I don't recognize them. They chomp at the bit to converse with me, but time waits for no Man. Perhaps they salivate to know the type of person I am, but why would I suffer myself to breach the notion that a prophet has no honor in his hometown?

Going in, you should be aware that a prophet is without honor in his hometown. That means that the more comrades and acolytes you have, the more honor is deprived from you. "Hometown," in this day and age doesn't mean your actual hometown. I was born in Ohio but I grew up in Calabar and Lagos, which are in Nigeria. And I have lived in New York since twenty-one years of age. I realize that regardless of what I have done, that is of no mean feat; my family, my friends and my neighbors (in towns in New York) seem to sneeze at or overlook my achievements, but a stranger who merely knows me and my accolades and achievements, never ceases from praising me.

Won't a prophet be a fool if he continues to preach to that choir? I have nothing of substance to say to my family and friends; lightening will not strike twice. This life is about God not about me so I wouldn't move heaven and earth for them to honor me. But nevertheless, the camaraderie exists between me and my people.

Jesus Christ was the first to utter the proverb, "A prophet is without honor in his hometown-" Matthew 13 verse 57. The wisdom of Jesus Christ can never satisfy this world. And I tell you the truth that the erudition of Man takes root from the Word of God.

Why would I prostitute myself to local people? Why would I unveil myself to local people when it's common sense that a prophet has no honor in his hometown? So long as they are not acquainted personally with me, my honor is retained. All praise belongs to God, but I'm not going to go around prostituting and losing my respect. I'm not going to be that big fish in a small pond. I would be dishonored by a thousand counts should I prostitute.

Tons of people have overwhelming respect for me because my appearance and the fear of God in me goes before me. By and large they are familiar with me but they can't approach me, so I'm not going to sell my honor down the river, lest at the end of the day, a prophet has no honor in his hometown.

If you sow you shall surely reap. Everybody loves to fornicate but nobody wants to bear the responsibility of the end product; thus a bastard is born to dead-beat parents, and the child is abandoned, adopted, or even killed. Every couple is happy for childbirth but nobody ceases from crying and lamenting when death occurs. They forget that there is a time for everything under the sun. Everybody calls on God when the going gets rough, but nobody wants to attend the tabernacle of God. Everybody prays as if everything depends on God, yet they act as if everything depends on Man. They make hypocrites of themselves. Everybody loves the pleasure of consuming but no one takes delight in excreting. Everybody loves the time to be remunerated but grudgingly accepts to work with joy. Nobody wishes to clean but everybody loves to use and abuse. Everybody loves to borrow but nobody wishes to refund, and when the lender comes for his due, the borrower gets an attitude. Everybody yearns to be told that they are beautiful, but ugliness is also in the eye of the beholder. Everybody loves strong drink but nobody wants to be called a drunkard. Everybody loves to smoke but if it results to cancer, blame no one but God. The aforementioned is all human nature.

How long have you (family and friends) been waiting and salivating to utter that disparaging and derogatory message to a loved one? How long have the words been on the tip of your tongue? There is no Man in this world, even your family and friends, who doesn't have any adverse comment they would utter about you. They just need to be provoked and the genie will be out of the bottle.

If you live by the Law of Moses then the Law of Moses will judge you, but if you live by the sufficient grace afforded by Jesus then the grace of God will judge you. An eye for an eye is the Law of Moses and turning the other cheek is the Gospel, which is the grace of God to those who believe. You can't have it both ways.

Ways of Man

I know all the ways of Man so I never put my trust in Man; I never hope and salivate for what Man swears in the name of God he will do for me. The ways of Man are the gesture, the behavior, and the language of Man.

The ways of Man are very easy to predict. But sometimes Man uses subliminal ways to conceal his intentions. You know you did or said something unbecoming, but when questioned, rather than apologize you get angry just to hide behind your fallings. Your anger becomes the elephant in the room. You get angry to justify your egregious action or you get angry to justify the action of your acquaintance. It's the height of righteous indignation in disguise.

In private and in a one-on-one conversation, you are willing to compromise and make all kinds of concessions. But in public, when people of your knit are around you, you do a three-sixty; hence, you no longer want to meet half way, you throw compromise out the window. At the end of the day, you are that stiff-necked pretender.

Why are there no miracles on earth like in the ancient days of old? If you come across a prophet that does miracles in and out of season, then be aware that there is something fishy about that so-called man of the cloth. You will smell a rat around the corner. Christ was able to do miracles because he was sinless.

Having the ability to perform a miraculous act is only given to a few; it's a gift from the Holy Spirit. Christ didn't suffer Himself to do miracles in His own hometown of Bethlehem because of the unbelief of Man. So miracles work both ways; the miracle will not manifest itself if the person at the receiving end of the prayer doesn't have the unshakable belief in the power of God. Apostle Excel has done manifold miracles; the greatest was that he raised a child from the dead by the power of God Almighty. Such types of miracles are a once-in-a-lifetime miracle. It's not a miracle that a prophet does on a regular basis.

Certain people, instead of taking responsibility for their failings, are fit to be tied and throw a tantrum and point fingers at everyone but themselves. But the buck stops with Adam since he blamed Eve for his downfall. Eve, in turn, blamed the serpent.

Testifying Against Oneself

You were a beggar on earth; hence, you discriminated against the rich. You hated the rich on the one hand, and on the other hand you blasphemed the name of God. And it came to pass that you assumed room temperature; you died as a beggar who disdained and execrated the name of God. You cursed the Potter for not making the clay the way you thought the clay ought to be made. Thus, you died and went straight to Hell. You experienced the worst of both worlds. You testified against yourself on earth.

For the most part, we can control the utterance from our mouths but we can't completely control what we see and what we hear. Inescapably, your eyes and your ears will judge you but you will forbid your mouth from judging you. There is no conceivable way you can forbid your eyes and your ears from judging you, but you can tame your mouth from judging you.

You wouldn't want to take back the things you said; you wouldn't want to eat your words—lest if you do, your mouth will judge you. You wouldn't want to boldly enunciate the truth, because you are scared of the power of the tongue. Life and death are in the power of the tongue.

He who has eyes let him see. Those eyes of yours will lead you to commit fornication; Christ said pluck them out. He who has ears let him hear. That ear of yours will refuse to heed to the Gospel of Jesus when it is preached. You will abjectly reject and deny yourself from harking to the Gospel; hence your ears will judge you.

Why should Man be *schadenfreude* and chomping at the bit to witness another man's downfall? Man curses at each other and is filled with envy, jealousy, and hatred against one another. Men are made to worship God, not made to fight and bicker among themselves. Why should a man betroth a woman and abuse her all the days of his wife's life?

Jamie Foxx called Barack Obama personal "Lord and savior." How many birds did he kill with one stone? Foxx, by and large, defiled the Holy Bible. Foxx blasphemed against Jesus Christ, even the Son of God. People who have uttered the phrase "personal Lord and Savior" have all been defiled by Foxx's egregious comments.

Intentionally calling a fellow sinful human being "personal lord and savior," is way beyond the pale. How long will God wink at men's ignorance, because calling a fellow sinful human being "personal Lord and savior" is a statement that Hell Fire condones. Eternal life or eternal damnation is in the power of the tongue; even in the power of the beholder's tongue.

If the Muslims are so radical for Allah or jihad, I'm very extreme for Jesus Christ. The only difference is that I don't desire blood as a penalty for someone's actions or utterances, but I desire the lake of fire as a penalty for those offenses.

Don't let earth be your Heaven, because you can't have it both ways. If earth is your Heaven, that means that life after death will be your eternal damnation. So don't suffer this earth to be your Heaven. Reject the pleasures of this world, unless you disregard the pleasure of Heaven, even the pleasure of eternal life. Don't let this world be your Heaven; don't live in Heaven on earth.

Rush Limbaugh is a good person and will be in Heaven because he is being hated by the world, the world has testified against him. So earth is not his Heaven; the kingdom of God will be Rush's Heaven—but like all men, he needs to fight for his salvation as it says in Philippians 2:12 "Work out your own salvation with fear and trembling."

You can't have two Heavens in this life. You can't live a flamboyant life on earth and still make it to God's kingdom of Heaven. You can't have two Heavens. The Kingdom of Heaven will testify against those that made earth their Heaven while on earth.

Heart of Man

You called yourself a man yet you wouldn't have anything to say because you are afraid of being raked over the coals, of being read the riot act, of being lambasted, of having aspersions cast upon you, and of upsetting the applecart. At the end of the day, although you are afraid of what Man can do to you, that doesn't prevent you from calling yourself a man.

You call yourself a man yet you don't want to be judgmental. Christ didn't back away from any question; He took the challenge of the Pharisees. You don't want to be criticized and humbled because you want to be accepted by the opposition. You don't want to be rightly controversial because you are afraid of being called names. A gutless coward who cowers in fear of Man is not a man.

Don't be scared of Man; be scared of the One who can condemn your soul and your body in the Lake of Fire, even the perpetual burning fire. Man can only killed the flesh. Enough said.

How could you call yourself a Man yet stop short of finishing your sentence? You don't utter what you really intend to say; you don't speak your mind because you are afraid of critics.

Finish the sentence and prove yourself the man that you claim to be. You call yourself a man yet you are scare to be tarred and feathered; you scare to take on all comers. I repeat—are you scared of what Man will do to you? You'd better repent because what Man will do to you is not even a microcosm or even a dry run of what the Lake of Fire will do to you eternally.

Only a paper tiger is scared to be censured. Because of what Man will think about you, you are scared to be known as a conservative Republican who condemns abortion. Because of what Man will say about you, you are scared to openly claim to be a Christian who wholeheartedly condemns homosexual marriage.

You'd better learn how to receive criticism here on earth because on Judgment Day, Satan, who is the accuser of the brethren, will enumerate before the Almighty God all the reasons why you should be dumped into the Lake of Fire. And if you refuse to surrender your life to Christ, mercy will be helpless to save you.

Would you rather knowingly deny the Son of God or would you rather betray the Son of God? Pick your poison. Everybody pees on Judas' grave because he betrayed Jesus, but everybody pampers Peter because there was only so much he could do in regards to denying Jesus Christ three times in the space of an hour. Before Peter abjectly denied Christ, he previously tried to prevent Christ from dying for the sins of all mankind when he removed a sword out of the sheath and cut off the ear of the high priest's servant. It's not about the beginning but it's all about the end; hence, at the end of the day, Judas Iscariot was the son of perdition and the Apostle Peter was a true servant of God, but in their lowest points there isn't much difference in what Judas did compared to what Peter did. There is a thin line between Heaven and Hell. At the beginning, Judas was designed to be a servant of the Devil while the Apostle Peter was designed to be the first preacher of Christianity, even the first Pope on earth. Everybody sings the praises of Peter and rakes Judas over the coals. Every man on earth has either betrayed or denied the Son of God.

And it came to pass that Paul happened to be homeless. And a stranger refused to accommodate him in his abode but his family friend accepted him. The stranger refused for Paul to stay with him but Paul's family friend welcomed Paul even with open arms. But how long is the family friend going to accommodate Paul in his home? How long is Paul going to tarry with the family friend? How long will the tarrying be tolerated? In the end, just as the stranger outrightly rejected Paul in the beginning, the family friend rejected Paul too. So who takes the cake, the one that rejected Paul upfront or the one that rejected Paul after they couldn't tolerate Paul any longer? And the latter (family friend) told the whole world how he nursed over Paul but he had to kick Paul out in order for Paul to pull himself up by his bootstraps. But the former (the stranger) knew that going in and didn't want to put on a show. So who takes the cake?

Don't start without finishing. Don't accommodate somebody and at the end of the day kick the person to the curb. If you can't cater for a beggar because you are incapable, God will take that beggar away from you even before you know it. Let the beggar leave on his own will, not on your own order.

Although John the Baptist was the forerunner for Jesus, Satan curtailed his vision. When he was incarcerated, John the Baptist questioned if Jesus was really the Christ or "should we look for another?" Satan put doubt in him; hence, John put his foot in his mouth. He was no longer certain that Jesus was the Christ; rather, there was a willing suspicion of disbelief about Christ. But before his death—before he was decapitated—his suspended reality was no longer an illusion.

We shouldn't dishonor a loved one who has died. When Paul was alive, you sang his praises; you ran out of compliments to render to Paul. But it came to pass that the beloved Paul died untimely, and you bewailed and mourned for days, even months. But there was only so much you could stomach. And you began regurgitating the immoral things that Paul did. Paul became a sermon that you used to preach about dishonor.

Relationships will never be the same; relationships will ebb, and as a result, bygones will take precedence. Bygones will never be bygones, water will not be allowed to be under the bridge, forgiving will never be forgetting, and it will never be the same. Yesterday's wrongs will creep in; it can only get worse; the more you know someone the less respect you have for them; a prophet has no honor in his or her hometown; and you could lie to yourself all day but denial is not just a river in Egypt.

Every day I'm always observing why my loved ones haven't yet rejected me. Life is a lesson. I knew every now and then that I would be rejected by my people, so I always go before rejection so as to cushion the harsh reality of rejection. I have all the wisdom in the world, so don't commiserate on me being rejected. Instead, pity yourself.

If I'm being complimented the best response is to say "thank God," because I don't want to be hornswoggled; I won't be deceived. If I get a compliment, I won't praise myself. I will praise God because I don't have the patience to ascertain if a compliment is genuine or not. Besides, should I try to ascertain if the compliment is under the guise or if it was borne from the heart, then I'm trying to claim the adulation for myself rather than claiming the adulation for God.

I detest calling myself a man because of the inhumane heart of Man.

Counsel

Who died and made me an adviser? It will cost an arm and a leg for me to render Man advice. My advice may not sit well with the readers, but like in the situation with Naomi and Ruth, God will send a questionable advice through a misfortunate, stricken person to a recipient. If people view me as an uncouth person or as a well-bred person, then my advice to that individual would either sound uncouth or sound well-bred.

Live a righteously planned life. Schedule daily appointments for yourself, lest out of left field the Devil will schedule and plan your days ahead for you. And you wonder why you are unceremoniously making a trip to the hospital. It's incumbent that you live a planned life; you should never live your life idle. Idle time will always be the Devil's workshop. Plan for what you will render to God tomorrow.

You shouldn't fail to utter the phrase "God willing" or "by God's grace" when addressing, referring to, or predicting the future—even if it is concerning five minutes from now—so that the grace of God will precede you. If you fail to do so, then you have made yourself to be God.

"People don't accept when you say you have change" from a terrible lifestyle, Apostle Excel once said. That saying is true and that is why it's incumbent to do the right thing all the time, lest you give Man the opportunity to accuse you of something flagrant, and so that you don't have to try to convince people that you have changed. God will accept that you have changed but Man will not. There will always be lingering doubts.

If Man's righteousness is a filthy rag before God, then what is Man's wickedness before God? As long as you do what is right, God will observe you. There is no reserved punishment for the righteous. But the punishment for the wicked culminates in the second death, even an everlasting damnation.

Don't shorten the hands of the Potter; in other words, let the sky be the limit. If Man is the limit then you have, by and large, shut God out of your life. So let the sky be the limit, not Man and his governing body.

It's absolutely common sense that if you live by the gun you will perish by the gun. In England guns are prohibited, but in America every man longs to be a legal and an illegal gun owner. Don't they have another think coming for them? What was Christ's take on weapons? Christ ordered His disciples to carry weapons in their possession. But on the other hand, Christ rebuked and reprehended Peter for using a weapon when Christ was on the verge of being apprehended. Christ was killing more than two birds with one stone. So Jesus intimated that even though He told you to bear a sword, He didn't authorize you to use it. In essence, one could license a gun but that doesn't mean that you should use it.

The only way to suppress any bad event that befalls you, you have to link it to God. If you refuse to do so, you will never have peace of mind. As soon as you link a devastating event to God, the restless and unsettledness will subside and gradually be quenched.

The world is coming to an end, so things can only get worse. If things seem to be better, then be aware that something drastic is on the horizon that will make up for those times that seem to be better. The world can only get worse because the world is coming to an end.

Before your life goes into abeyance, give your life to Jesus, now that your life is in progress. Don't put it off for tomorrow because someone is guaranteed to assume room temperature tomorrow. And there is no telling that it won't be you. Live every day on earth as if it's your last day; put your house in order each and every passing day. Ask for the forgiveness of your sins and the sins of your household. Job stood in the gap for his children; he offered sacrifices for the sins that his ten children had perhaps committed against God. Job did so because he knew the nature of man. But at the end of the day, Job buried all of the first set of ten children he begot. And it begs the question: Were Job's sacrifices to God in vain? God is a respecter of no man; God is a respecter of no sin.

We have to live a surrendered life. If I get slapped by someone by no fault of mine, God sent that person to slap me. They are a servant of God, albeit ignorantly. I live my life every step of the way by God the Holy Spirit. The Holy Spirit goes before me every day. If you surrender yourself wholeheartedly to God then everything that befalls you is God's will. The Holy Spirit will abide with you in totality. If you believe that everything happens for a reason, then you must believe that the reason is from God and God only. But should you tempt the Holy Spirit by premeditatedly asking for peoples' trouble, then the culmination of what befalls you wouldn't be the working of the Holy Spirit. If you put God first in everything you do and God goes before you, the ambush on the horizon and the accident waiting to happen will be deterred and countered by the Lord because you suffered the Lord to go before you.

In my world

I consider myself an English person but I was elected to be born in Ohio, even in Cleveland. My parents, being from Nigeria, count me as a Nigerian too. Christ is my Master and I would maintain that as Christ was elected to be born in Bethlehem but was from Heaven, so I too who am a servant of the Almighty God, was elected to be born in Cleveland but was from the foundation of the world.

Am I a fool that I live in the greatest country in the world and yet I don't live in New York City? Am I a fool that I live in the New York City suburbs rather than in the city? I live in the city of New York where God has found me a habitat, even in Brooklyn. Is everywhere else in America not a step backward, even in the Stone Ages, compared to New York City?

The kings of Israel, the prominent and the noble men, were they living in some remote city in Israel or were they living in Jerusalem? Even Jesus, when He came to this world, lived many times in Jerusalem.

What am I doing living in the cities of Texas, California, Florida, or any other city in America? Am I a fool? Isn't Texas, California, Florida, and the rest of the states in America dead ends compared to New York? New York City is the greatest. I wouldn't be caught dead living in any city in America unless the Lord puts a gun to my head. I have nostalgic feelings every time I leave New York to go to any other place in the world, even to London. In Luke 9 verse 38, Christ said, "Foxes have holes, and birds of the air have nests; but the Son of Man hath not where to lay his head," so what will I be doing living in remote places like Texas, Florida, or California? In New York you live everyday as if it were your last day. A day in New York is like a week in Texas. I wouldn't be caught dead living in Florida. New Yorkers are furtively speaking, a den of thieves, and there is honor among thieves. There is respect among fellow New Yorkers, but not so much for outsiders.

My attitudes and shortcomings are an open book to me and I move heaven and earth to make sure they are not perceived by Man. No man can reveal something about me which I don't already know. I have taken the mote out of my eyes.

No one can pull me aside and relate something about me that I'm not aware of. If a man detects something shrewd about me, then I will take my hat off to that person. But since a prophet has no honor in his hometown, I don't try to hide certain of my attitudes and shortcomings to certain acquaintances.

If I don't deceive, steal, or fornicate, then I am the epitome of a perfect man. If I worship God every day of my life then I am the greatest thing since sliced bread; if I wholeheartedly acknowledge and confess my iniquities before God every hour of the day that I am awake, then I am the envy of the world. If I do the right thing all the time and the Word of God is ever before me, then I am the be-all and end-all. And although I put my pants on one leg at a time, I am specially made and the mold that made me has long been broken.

People view me mysteriously. People generally are scared of me; they are not frightened in frozen fear of me but scared as in not sure of who I really am. Because I am out rightly peculiar, a different breed which they have never witnessed before, I seldom do the things that people in general do. Although I have never done anything untoward to harm any man in this life, they are still not sure about me; they still can't asseverate and vouch for me without a degree of doubt. They can't anticipate or predict my ways, but my ways are not hidden, neither are they secretive. My ways are extremely real. And being a Rush Limbaugh conservative only adds fuel to the fire.

In my world, we are real; we are absorbed in reality. "The way things ought to be," Rush Limbaugh said. Living a real lifestyle is spontaneous and unstudied to me. Rush Limbaugh talked about being the mayor of "Realville." It's difficult for people to be real because the real will feel like it's being tested. Everything about me is real; realness is inherent in me.

In my world, you are guilty until proven innocent. And the road to proving of innocence is so grave and onerous that you would rather accept being found guilty for the rest of your life than to fight to be found innocent. Hence, you have Rush Limbaugh who is hated by the whole country because he espouses the truth in and out of season.

In my world, we can surely forgive but we can't forget. If we say we can forget it means we are lying to ourselves. Bygones will surely be bygones, but bygones will first have to be judged and pardoned. In my world, when you fail, you don't give up. You pull yourself up by your bootstraps. In my world, Caesar's wife must be above suspicion.

In my world we are true; we are guided by the truth. True means original, the way it ought to be; no abortion and homosexual marriage is tolerated. In my world we are holy sinners. God urged Man to be holy. And when you happen to be holy, the world will excoriate you for trying to be "too holy" even holier than God. "Too holy" is not in the thought of the beholder, rather is in the thought of the jealous party.

I live in my own world, a world where only sin is the common denominator with the rest of the world. A world close to God's original plan for Man in His perfect will for Man before Adam failed and fell. A world where everybody admits that fornication, homosexual marriage, etc. is wrong and not tolerated in any way, shape, or form. As soon as you disagree or compromise in my world, you will be ostracized and kicked out quicker than Adam and Eve were kicked out of the Garden of Eden. You have turned back and you might not become salt like Lot's wife, because my world is not a guaranteed ticket to heaven.

Even in my own world, I'm in my own league. I'm the epitome of the smallest minority. I don't want or seek to tell people what to do. Generally speaking, I don't like human beings in the first place. But what is the meaning of "like" in this context? Lucifer wanted to build his throne above the throne of the Almighty. Lucifer was drunk with power. I can't be like Lucifer because I hate the idea of ruling over people. It's too easy to rule over people. Individually, human beings are just outright ignorant and void of wisdom. To be a boss over people is an enemy to me. It's above my pay grade. If I had to rule over people I would be pretending and I don't live a pretentious life. But I tell you that the Holy Spirit has imparted me with wisdom above any other wisdom on earth. Even though I'm sufficient, I continue to beseech God for more wisdom every day of my life because His wisdom is infinite.

I defend those who are wrongfully maligned and vilified; that is the reason why generally I defend Whites over Blacks because the cry for racism against Blacks is blown out of proportion. We concur that the first thing in the mind of typical Blacks upon seeing Caucasians is that Whites are racists? Blacks could beg to differ and deny lying to themselves, but they can't lie to their heart. And if tomorrow the shoe is on the other foot, then I will defend the Blacks over the Whites.

I'm a defender of the rich, because certain ones have no love lost for the rich. And I'm a defender of conservatives because conservatism is hated worldwide. Remember that I'm the individual, the smallest minority, so I'm a defender of those who are vastly hated by the world.

Sean Hannity said, "Live a straight and narrow life; live a moral and reclusive life."

Sean Hannity is my ilk; Hannity is prominently part of my world.

I have no mortal enemy; no human being could ever be an enemy of mine.

Characters

I have a cynical view on everything about Man. I believe the worst about Man. I disparage the worth of Man. There is nothing pleasant and gratifying about a man who doesn't believe in God.

Can I be counted as a man? A man is known by the company he keeps. I don't keep company; all of my friends are of yesteryear. I'm withdrawn and somewhat antisocial. I'm like a fish out of water when I am in public places—behind enemy lines, if you will. I have to make myself seldom seen and unreachable. I live a private but not secretive lifestyle. I am a person that, where I'm known in public places, I'm the epitome of a divided opinion. I'm the epitome of the smallest minority. There are no birds of the same feather that I flock with.

I believe in sex only after marriage and I'm not speaking against fornication or against whoredom because I have repented from those acts or because I once lived a promiscuous lifestyle. I'm speaking as an abstinent Christian. The risk inherent in fornication and in adultery as a whole is grave.

I have lived in the greatest city in the world for over a decade, yet I have never womanized. I disclose this with pride that God has not counted me among womanizers and prostitutes of the world. I'm God's reserved in a city of abominations. I live in New York City and I am not incognito by any stretch of the imagination, yet I have never tasted strong drinks. I say this with pride that God has not counted me among the drunkards of the world, neither has He numbered me among the smokers of the world. It's no mean feat.

As a conservative pundit, I am a stuffed shirt because I greatly abhor liberalism in any way, shape, or form. As a Christian I'm a humble person, and as a friend I am subliminal.

All my identities don't intercross. For example, as a conservative writer or pundit, I don't spew in support of the poor, but as a Christian I do give alms to the poor. And as a friend I play devil's advocate in why should or why shouldn't the destitute be succored.

Playing devil's advocate is part and parcel of my life. Playing mind games and using reverse psychology tactics are characteristics of my subliminal nature. I play devil's advocate to test Man's wisdom for the most part.

My utterances are mainly idioms, proverbs, and figurative language, so as to avoid relating the full meaning of a message. There is more than meets the eye in everything about me. Don't ponder what I do on face value. You will be hoodwinked. Just about every message I send is a subliminal message. My messages are not predicated on falsehood or deceit; it kills many birds with one stone.

To kill one bird with one stone to me is a waste of precious time; it's idle time. If one stone (action or utterance) kills many birds, which birds that I killed do you want me to explain? Because I have a hatful of reasons for what I did for the stone I catapulted. If I killed one bird with one stone then it would be predictable for Man to ascertain the reason of what I did or said; it would be predictable for Man to ascertain the one bird that was killed. But if I killed a hatful of birds with one stone, opinions will run the gamut; Man will not certainly know why I did or said what I did or said. Man will never be satisfied with me. Man will never understand me; hence, he will always read me wrong. I'm all about substance. So if I killed a hatful of birds with one stone in my utterance or action, it has to be substantive. It's part of my lifestyle. To me the realization of killing many birds with one stone is not a realization of innocence or a realization after the event.

I'm the most difficult person in this world to deal with. Anything you devise against me, make sure you take your best shot, because it could be your last. Certain people will shoot first and ask questions later. But I will shoot first and shoot again later. No time for conversation.

If I'm certain that what I believe in is rooted in the truth and nothing but the unadulterated truth, there is no way in Hell that I can even entertain the contrary. I'm not going to agree with someone who believes in a hoax or a lie. Neither am I going to find some type of middle ground.

I refuse to prostitute and commonize the wisdom that God bestowed upon me; I won't bring myself down to appease people. By virtue of my God-given wisdom, I'm a leader; hence, I can't be a follower to a fellow leader who is a mortal, only the leader that is the Holy Spirit. I can't subordinate or dismiss my ideology over another man's ideology. The only ideology that eclipses mine is the Gospel of Jesus Christ. Even though I'm a proud Limbaugh conservative, I am in a league of my own. I'm at a depth that can't be reached.

The world and his wife all maintain that I am very stubborn, so I guess if the shoe fits, I should wear it? I'm only stubborn to Man because there is nothing substantially left to learn from Man. And I'm a man of substance. I'm a thorn to mankind.

On the surface, I'm a gentleman; but if Man tries to bite more than he can chew, then I become a difficult person to deal with. But should I get insulted or disrespected, then I morph into the most difficult person to deal with. And my difficulties are met with an unmeasured amount of seriousness.

There is no one on earth like me—not yesterday, not today, and surely not tomorrow, because of the infinite wisdom God has bestowed on me. It's incumbent for me to make certain that there are no similarities between me and Man. If there is one iota of similarity between me and Man then it mustn't be perceive by Man. And the term "similarity" is not in the thought of observers (Man); rather, it is in the thought of the beholder (me). I don't want to be mistaken for or like someone else. I am in a league of my own. I'm not the one who gives someone an attitude because something doesn't sit well with me. The last thing I want is to be identified by a physical attitude. I only want to be identified by my writings and the words that proceed out of my mouth.

Christ snubbed the Canaanite woman who begged Him to make whole her sick daughter. Christ did not come for the Gentiles but for the lost sheep of Israel. Christ wasn't snubbing for snubbing's sake. Christ initially snubbed the Canaanite woman because He was relating a subliminal message, an eternal message. Every message that Christ addressed killed more than two birds with one stone. I don't have it in my heart to snub people; if I disregard people it is because everybody has gone astray from the Word of God. If I'm a stuffed shirt is because people are morally corrupt.

Because I'm a conservative Christian I can't restrain people from thinking dissentingly about me. Because I loathe Man's behavior I can't repress people from thinking antagonistically about me. More power to their elbow to think contrary about me. But I wouldn't let people think negatively of me because I'm a cheat or because I owe Man a debt. So when I deal with people, I deal justly.

Doing the right thing is a choice you have to make. I live in the heart of New York City; almost everybody around me is of immoral behavior, but I'm the contrary. It's all about choice; it's all about the Word of God within me. And because I am not damaged goods, neither am I defiled, I get lots of flak from acquaintances. They regard me as a weirdo—weird because I choose to be moral and just. I have been reserved by God.

I don't want God Almighty to view me the way He views a fornicator or a proponent of homosexual marriage, etc. When God said He looked down to see if there were any that truly seek after Him, I want to be that one exception. Everybody wants what is pleasant in their eyes regardless of whether it's morally right or wrong.

I have to live a pretentious life when associating with people. People in general are mediocre; hence, when I hear someone say something smart I will laud that person to the hilt. I can't associate with people and at the same time be serious; I would go crazy and nobody would be able to stand me. And with the infinite wisdom God has bestowed upon me, if I am charismatic, then there is absolutely no way I could be serious when dealing with Man.

I'm a straight shooter; I never reserve what I need to say. The truth is the truth—I'm not going to compromise on that. The moment you compromise the truth you have denied God. I would rather not comment or get involved if the issue doesn't sit well with me. Compromise is one of my biggest adversaries.

When Jesus was asked about the question of authority, He exemplified that it's not mandatory for us to answer all the questions being asked. If you refuse to believe in God then you must believe and agree with Satan. If you don't believe my word which stem from the truth, then you agree with the untruth.

I'm not better than any man in this world but I hate prostituting; I hate making myself common; hence, it would be an abomination if the mystical, local, common people in the neighborhood are acquainted with me, because at the end of the day a prophet has no honor in his hometown. We have to pass through Jesus Christ in order for us to see Almighty God. You have to labor extremely hard before you could personally know me.

I don't know how to curse my loved ones and even my acquaintances; I don't have time to learn how to use profanity and vulgarity on that front. I'm original and my bloom will never be off the rose.

I'm way beyond being deceived by Man. So being nice to people doesn't translate to being stupid. When it comes to my true people that God has assigned me, love trumps wisdom. I forsake wisdom in the back and thrust love to the forefront. I can't be beguiled by Man also because I already have a cynical view of Man. I have to deceive myself first in order to make Man think he has succeeded in deceiving me.

I don't compete with mortals; I don't look at people's progress and betterment in order to compare it to mine or try to measure how far I am compared to them. Competition will always be an enemy to me.

God bless the Potter for making me diminutive. The clay can't tell the Potter how he should be made. And because of that, I won't be caught dead acting and behaving like man. I won't be mistaken for another man because I rebuff the pleasures of the world.

People don't really respect me because I'm diminutive. A section of people think I'm a maniac because I lost an eye. But none of them possess half the wisdom that I have. To those who know me, there is no honor for a prophet in his hometown. I don't yearn for Man's respect because God has bestowed upon me invincible wisdom. Wisdom trumps respect; pure wisdom is from God while respect is from Man. But God is a no respecter of Man, so go figure. For people who don't respect me because of jealousy and envy, I maintain that I certainly don't need their respect and it will be an absolute insult to me if those particular people have respect for me.

I never commonized myself for any man except the One who created me. No man can get on this level and status that I am on; it's an unattainable and invincible level. I don't participate in small— or large-scale idle talk, gossip, or rumors; no man is worthy to be gossiped about. It wasn't written in the stars that I should commonized myself for Man. If I make myself common for my missing rib, well, we are one flesh and one blood; I only make myself common for the Almighty Father.

I don't insult nor do I hurl expletives at people, because if you don't believe in Jesus Christ you have a bigger curse than what I would utter. Hence, there is no need to utter epithets and double entendre toward people, lest God might repent of His disciplining them if I had to resort to cursing people.

I'm all about the greatest. A man can't save a man; it's only Jesus who can save Man. So I don't fancy the story of the Virgin Mary and John the Apostle, etc. I'm only hook, line, and sinker invested in the true story of Jesus.

I'm bar none the greatest force on earth that Man will ever reckon with; hence, I'm the most difficult person Man will contend with. As a result of being so invincible, everybody and their uncle have concluded that I'm stubborn-minded. But in order for you to retain the truth and not let an iota of truth escape from you, then you must certainly be intractable to Man.

Ignorance Is Bliss

If you utter the phrase "I will go shopping tomorrow" without finishing the sentence, then you have made yourself equal to God. You have demanded parity with God. "By the grace of God I will go shopping tomorrow" implies that you are acknowledging that there is no guarantee that you will splurge tomorrow, but that if you will splurge tomorrow, it will be because of God's grace.

Referring to the future without uttering "by the grace of God," is a sin of ignorance. But the Bible says in Acts 17:30, "And the times of this ignorance God winked at, but now commandeth all men everywhere to repent."

Blacks—African Americans particularly—predominately believe that Jesus was a Black Man. If we give them the benefit of the doubt that Jesus was a Black Man, at the end of the day that notion would not guarantee them a place in Heaven if they didn't repent of their sins. They wouldn't be regenerated if they didn't totally yield themselves to God. To even classify Christ as either Black or White is a sin in itself.

There is no ignorance in terms of colorblindness. If you are not colorblind, then you are a racist. And being a racist doesn't make you ignorant. So you can't claim innocence. You can't profess to be ignorant in regards to colorblindness.

African Americans have been deceived by firebrand activists that fighting against Whites is a just cause. It's not their battle to fight against Whites. If Blacks want to avenge the Whites for their host of grievances, then Blacks have taken matters into their own hands. They have become their own God. They complain about Blacks being lynched. If they don't believe that God has already punished those who committed lynching, then they will surely not believe that God has punished the White slave owners. So since their appetite is not satisfied, they continuously want to take matters in their own hands. Blacks want to condemn Whites; they want Whites to be executed, and only then will their appetite be satisfied. Only then will their dream be fulfilled.

Before Blacks realize it, their final dwelling place lies where the evil slave owners and those who perpetrated the lynching are, at the deepest depth of Hell. Ancient slavery history keeps getting repeated to the younger generation, indoctrinating Black youngsters to unceasingly hate Whites, and all the inhumane stories that Blacks have absorbed about what the White man perpetrated, have gotten Blacks all breathing out murder for the Whites. Hence, bygones will never be bygones. Hence, listening and reading about the abominable acts committed against the Blacks will lead them to Hell. It's not as if they witnessed first-hand what the Whites did to the Blacks; no, it was told to them by august Black agitators. Hence, the Black rabble-rousers are leading the Black youth to Hell Fire. Just as Christ said, the Pharisees are preventing the Jews from salvation because they themselves are already doomed. They are dragging their fellow Black brothers to Hell Fire by indoctrinating them to hate the Whites.

Blacks are hell-bent and consumed in fighting the physical battle of the flesh while living on earth, instead of fighting the spiritual battle of eternal salvation. They have forgotten that all human beings are children of Noah and originally children of Adam. And Adam's first son slayed Adam's second son. So what is the difference between Cain killing Abel and a White killing a Black during slavery? And which hurt the most, a brother killing a brother or a total stranger killing a total stranger?

If you live in the flesh you will die in the flesh and you will never understand spiritual things. If African American men of the cloth and prophets live a material and an earthly life, they only serve to corrupt their congregation. You have fallen prey to hatred and enmity for the Whites. The worst thing a man can do to you is kill you, but a man can't grant eternal life to you. The million-dollar question for certain Blacks is: Do you want to reiterate and avenge the White man by killing him, hence making it to Hell Fire in perpetual burning? Or do you want to be killed by the White man (which was yesterday during slavery) and make it to Heaven? The water is already under the bridge, so let bygones be bygones.

Christ has impeccably paved the way for your salvation but you continue to fight against the flesh. You are fighting against Heaven and against your salvation if you continue to harbor hatred against Whites and those who you consider as foes. But African American elders, demagogues, and instigators are constantly breathing out threats and slaughtering against the Whites. But if you remind them that it was their own brothers who sold them to the White man, they would not be willing to entertain such questions. African Americans realize their dream when White people get killed.

God will judge us according to our wisdom and according to our ignorance.

Colorblind

Why do we choose a Black over White or vice versa? Love your neighbor as you love yourself, but you love those of the same skin color as yourself more than you love the ones of a different skin color. And if you happen to be a Christian then aren't you a hypocrite? The Black population supports and champions a Black over a White because it has animosity toward Whites.

If Satan puts on black skin, Blacks will still cast their lot for a Black over a White—even though they had been severely warned that underneath the skin is evil. Ignorance runs the gamut. Skin is just a deceiver.

Jesus Christ's commandments are by and large preached to every generation. His commandment is the colorblind commandment, "Love your neighbor as you love yourself-" Matthew 22 verse 39. For those who reside or sojourn in a racial society, Christ's commandments leave no stone unturned.

The reason why I greatly loathe Man's attitude and behavior in general is because Man refuses to be colorblind. Man chose to be racist, bigoted, prejudiced, etc. Man hates White people because of slavery. Men are race-baiters. Man is prejudiced against Blacks because Adam was African. On the colorblind front, no Man wants to sing from the same hymn sheets.

I thank God for making me colorblind. I thank God for not suffering me to choose a Black over a White, or vice versa. There is no windfall in lying to myself. I have been called rotten names because I'm a Black conservative.

From the onset, God chose all my loved ones for me so I must love them more than strangers. If my real brother Ntiense is the one that I love the most in this life, of course I will choose him over any man on the face of the earth. But to choose a generic Black over a generic White because of skin color is incongruous.

Either a man is racist or a man is colorblind. There are no two ways about it. If I were elected by God to judge people, will a racist, anti-Semite, or a chauvinist make it to the kingdom of God? But God is holy, holy is His name. I'm a sinner. My righteousness is mingled with iniquity. The fact that I'm colorblind is a sin before God.

By God's enlightenment, my message on earth is to preach colorblindness to those whom God ought to save for His kingdom. Bifurcating due to race or tribe is wrong. If you are Black, let your love for Whites whom God has put in your path be within and without, in public and in private. Let that be your true color and we will all be singing from the same hymnal. Let Man not be a party to racism and bigotry. Let Man not be an accessory to racial, tribal, or religious prejudice. Ask yourself this question: If today you are Black and you race-bait against Caucasians, if tomorrow by divine intervention you become Caucasian, would you still race-bait against Caucasians? Has skin color taken precedence over righteousness? Thus, your true colors are revealed.

A colorblind society would be an ideal society—but that would be utopia. If certain Blacks cast their lot for a Black over a White, or vice versa, solely because the individual looks like them, then they have counted themselves as fools. The language of skin color is the language of Hell Fire. The language of "someone looks like me" is the language of the bottomless pit. I don't care if you are White or Black—if you believe in Christ, I love you, but if you don't, you are of the son of perdition. And you have nothing in me.

Your Neighbors

Nobody loves their neighbor like they love themselves. Don't hate and discard a racist, chauvinist, or anti-Semite neighbor of yours because God has placed them along your way for His reason. Why rub shoulders with people, if after all is said and done, they are racist, bigoted, chauvinistic, and prejudiced toward others? I don't get involved in what, at the end of the day, is vain. I don't live a vain life.

Discrimination and prejudice are inborn in all human beings; there is a measure of discrimination and prejudice in Man, but don't be prejudiced because of society. Let the discrimination inborn in you be natural. It's natural to love your offspring more than other people's offspring; let that be the only discrimination in you. Catastrophic and tragic events like slavery and the Holocaust only serve to intensify division among us; they only serve to cause discrimination, racism, bigotry, and prejudice. We are all fashioned in God's image but only those who believe in God are fulfilled in God's image. God chose Israel as His people; God didn't seem to care about any other race or nation. So let's try to be like God in that fashion. Let's truly love and cherish those whom God has predetermined and put on our path. And as for the rest of the people in the world, God will cater for them. He is the Potter.

If you can't find it in your heart to love those people who are given to you that you behold, how can you love the people of the world? It's a fantasy. If God chose Israel and rejected Moab, the Philistines, etc., it happened for a reason. It happened because God said to love your neighbors as you love yourself. Conservatives and Christians are my elect, while my people (family and friends) are my blood.

If I assert and endeavor to show publicly that I love people of all ages, races, faith—by and large, mankind as a whole—then I'm attempting to build my throne above the throne of the Almighty God. And if I go further to say that I'm not biased toward any man then I'm claiming to be God Almighty. Christ confessed that the world is against Him, so He only prayed for those who God has kept for Him. By and large, God is not a God for all people. God is not all things to all men but God provides for all people (the wicked and the righteous) because they are the work of His hands; they are the clay and He is the Potter. And God has given them (the righteous and the wicked) a path to salvation, which is to believe in Jesus Christ.

How difficult was it for Jesus to work with Judas Iscariot for three straight years? We all have devils in our lives and we have to deal with them until the end of this life. A Judas could be your neighbor but don't loathe them because Jesus didn't hate Judas Iscariot.

If you are a Black who lives in a White neighborhood or vice versa, then the commandment of Jesus Christ will put you to the test. You have to love your neighbor as yourself; that is the nuts and bolts of Christ's commandment. It's all about colorblindness. The end result of slavery was to pit Blacks against Whites, and if you fall for the end result, then you have failed Jesus' commandments. Ignorance will no longer be bliss.

The Word of God doesn't state that you should love the world as you love yourself, but it states, "Love your neighbor as you love yourself." Don't brood over poverty in Africa, Asia, etc., because there is nothing you can do—even your donation and charity is vanity upon vanity. Love your neighbors; the people in Africa and Asia are not your neighbors if you reside in America. How many beggars are you familiar with on your way to work and on your way to merchandizing? Those panhandlers are your neighbors.

Slavery, discrimination, genocide, lynching, beheading, racism, etc.—think of the worst thing that a man can do to you. At the end of the day, we live in God's world; God knows what is happening on earth. Slavery, discrimination, genocide, lynching, beheading, and racism are all servants of God. And it all has to do with loving your neighbor as you love yourself.

Time Is of the Essence

People are dying every second of every given day, so listen to what the time is telling you to do. Listen attentively to the time so that the time will listen to your prayers and meditation.

But if you seek the way of the whores and eventually commit all kinds of abominable acts, then you are not listening to the time. You are harking to the wages of sin.

Time is of the essence, so there is no time to delay; there is no time to kick the can down the road; there is no time to tread water; there is no time for compliancy; and there is no time to rest on one's laurels because people are passing away by the second.

While men sleep, the enemy will always sow tares. But the bush has ears and the moon could run, but the day will eventually catch it. We have to pray without ceasing. Time is of the essence, so be sure to know the tares which the adversary has planted among the wheat.

People are dying every given second yet you choose to deal with trivial and insignificant things. There is no time to wait after the events to be clever because time is of the essence. You are trying to know the difference between an abomination and gay marriage.

What is the difference between supporting abortion and wishing death upon someone?

What is the difference between living by the gun and being a victim of a gun crime by an intruder? What is the difference between someone who does not believe that Jesus is the Son of God and a fool? Is there any difference between having a concubine and being married? Is there any difference between a single unmarried mother and a prostitute? Perhaps there is a difference but it pales into insignificance in comparison; it's irrelevant in the grand scheme of things because people are dying every second.

There is no time to beat around the bush and there shouldn't be time for idle tale, because people are dying every second. Time is of the essence, so I would not kill one bird with one stone. People die every second, so I wouldn't go a day without worshiping God. Cursed be the Devil who will try for that day to be conceived.

The sand is running out of the hourglass, so I wouldn't get into heated arguments and fights with people because people assume room temperature every second. Liberal policies and schemes make me ill, so I wouldn't listen to liberals prevaricate when poverty is prevalent in Africa and Asia, etc. All your time spent on earth will be judged.

Patience might be a virtue but a five-minute waste of my time is the same as a one or more hour waste of my time to me. I'm always in a rush because I know too much. There are twelve hours in a day, but because of my overwhelmingly busy lifestyle, would to God that there were forty-eight hours in a day. But if it were so, would that still be sufficient? Idle time is my worst enemy; idle time is the devil's workshop. It is sin to me.

Lost in Translation

I have come in for heavy criticism throughout my adult life. Detractors tarred and feathered me because of my principal beliefs. I don't hesitate to turn the other cheek when detractors call me names. Aren't feathers meant to be ruffled? A prophet is not without honor except in his own hometown, whether it is in Calabar, London, or New York.

I'm a spiritual fellow, so denigration, defamation, insults, name calling, and character assassinations hurled against me are compliments. They hold no weight; they are dead upon arrival. My life is about the truth so I ignore all the criticism. It comes with the territory.

Dissenters lay in wait to give me a piece of their mind. I have been called rotten names because of being a Black unadulterated conservative. And because of my constant opposition to liberal policies, certain acquaintances have said they would have slain me if I were living in their native country. And I don't take their comments lightly. Dissenters claim that I'm a racist against my own race. Calling me a whiter-than-white Uncle Tom who has sold his race down the river is an everyday thing; but I can stand the heat, so I'm no time soon getting out of the kitchen. You have situations in which acquaintances wake up on the wrong side of the bed, sucking lemon and approached me with mouth dripping with disdain.

The outrageous and hideous statements people have hauled against me are beyond the pale. They are unutterable, so I categorize them as lost in translation.

In closing, I savor the things of God, not the things of Man. As a result, I can't be serious in the things of Man, but in the things of God I'm gravely serious, like in my worship of God. I endeavor to be serious in the things of Man, but it's just not in me. I saw Rush Limbaugh live in person, so they only Being left and worthy for me to see is Jesus Christ.

Man tailors the words of God to suit his wrong doings. He misinterprets and doctors the Word of God to justify his wrong deeds. God is not mocked. We have been equipped with common sense to distinguish right from wrong.

Because of men's despicable acts I would rather die than to be like any human being ever created in this world.

It's human nature for Man to change when the going gets tough; when he can no longer keep his head above water. The ways of Man has ceased to amaze me. The heart of Man is hardened beyond measure. My comments about Man cut way too close to the quick, but the truth is the truth; to compromise on the truth is to condone and accept Man's wicked ways. Beware of those that are adjudged to be good because their hearts are far away from righteousness. No man is good except the One who died on the cross. I don't hate human beings, I just hate the sin not the sinner—the sin being the language, ideology, attitude, etc. I have been demonized time without number for being a Neanderthal, an ultra-conservative. Having said that, I'm too charismatic that I can't possibly be hated. And if there is animosity toward me, at the end of the day, no man can openly vouch for hating me.

If the Holy Spirit was a sinful man I would blasphemy against Him every day of my life. Apostle Excel once said to me that I will be greater than him. But I'm not trying to be like Man. I have denied myself as a man. I have carried the cross and I'm on the road to Calvary and behold I see millions of people on the road to Damascus, even the road to the abyss. I'm watching all of you; I'm watching all of mankind.

Chapter 6

Cherub

———— ⌒⌒⌒⌒⌒⌒ ————

Covering Cherub

I'm a covering cherub. God has made me the greatest force on earth that Man will ever reckon with. I'm an observer of what isn't happening. I'm a double-edged sword and the last vestige of truth.

I'm a covering cherub. I beseeched the Lord in a prayer, asking if I'm like Lucifer before iniquity was found in him. I quizzed the Lord if I was made in the mold of Lucifer. I can't be like Man. Man possesses stale wisdom. Man has nothing on me. Behold, I have seen the end of the wisdom of Man. Behold, I know all the ways of Man.

A prophet is not without honor, save in his hometown. But certain people will not believe me because their heart has been permanently hardened. God bestowed on Lucifer the greatest anointing, but Lucifer used it for evil against the Word of God. God has anointed me with an enviable anointing. And I used it for wisdom for the Word of God. Lucifer was created "perfect in beauty." His beauty was second to none.

God fashioned a perfect beauty upon me like He did for Lucifer but Lucifer took away one of my eyes and God transferred the perfect beauty He gave me to a perfect wisdom. Lucifer went down from Heaven swinging; he made certain that the beauty that God fashioned me with was made tarnished. Even while I was a child, I was in the crosshairs of Lucifer; Lucifer aided and abetted in taking my right eye. I was only seven years old when Satan took my eye. Since Lucifer took half of my beauty away via the lost eye, God perfected my wisdom. So the loss of half of my beauty was complimented with a perfect comprehensive wisdom.

Lucifer took a third of the angels when he was cast down from Heaven. And he swore to win converts to Hell Fire, even to Hades. I'm a one-man army; I was created and appointed to win converts to the kingdom of God. Hence, nothing in this material world is mine.

I was created specifically to supersede Lucifer on earth; that is why I can't live this life without worshiping God. I wondered why I had the deepest sincere desire to praise God with songs and hymns all the time, and I realize that it is because I'm a cherubim.

I liken myself to Lucifer before iniquity was found in him. I'm not even comparing myself to great men like Abraham, Moses, and Elijah; I'm not fond of Man. For all intents and purposes, God is done with Man as a whole. Since Christ came and died for the sins of Man, there is nothing left in the card for God to do for mankind. Man is left to his own devices. Man is left to strive for his own salvation. And remember that the defeat of Lucifer is the last battle to be fought before the world comes to an end. Man's days are numbered on earth as soon as he is born, but Lucifer's days are until the end of time. And if I am all about the foremost, then I am all about the climax; Man is anticlimactic while Lucifer is climatic. Death will be defeated on the last day, not Man.

One of the ways that I observe what is not happening is when I observe why the Devil is not tempting me; I'm always observing why Satan is not tempting me in a situation. I observe Satan working in people especially during people's idle time. I observe how Satan uses people as his tool. And I nod my head. Satan isn't even ashamed that I perceive and behold the damage that he does to someone nearby.

I was born as a human being but I have morphed spiritually into a cherubim or a seraphim. People laugh me to scorn when I insist that I'm not human. Differentiating and demarcating myself from mankind has only led to heavy criticism; the obvious being "you think you are better than us." I'm different because no stone goes unturned; the truth about all the ways of Man will be unearth and exposed.

So Satan who took my eyes didn't know that God will use the damaged eye to bless me. God used my infirmities to bless me with an invincible towering wisdom.

Greatest Force to Reckon With

God has made me the greatest force any Man will ever reckon with on earth. God anointed me while I was unborn. For that reason Satan fought tooth and nail to take my life when I was only about three years of age, but he ended up taking my innocent brother's life. I liken myself to Lucifer, that archangel, even the son of the morning, but when he was perfect, when iniquity wasn't found in him, and before he was cast down from Heaven. A mortal can't be an enemy of mine; I wouldn't afford Man that opportunity and that prestige and honor to be an enemy of mine. Lucifer remains my one and only enemy in this life.

Man's despicable acts, coupled with my towering wisdom, have made me lose all respect for Man. But because God said "honor thy father and mother," the only respect I have for Man is greetings. But although I have lost all respect for men I would never suffer myself to disrespect any man in this world.

On a regular basis, my acquaintances excoriate me and read me the riot act. They take turns in chastising me and conspire in trying to put a nail in the coffin so as to defile the notion of me distinguishing myself from Man. But their desire never saw the light of day.

Impugning, maligning, name calling, and character assassinations hurled against me are compliments to me. And lauding, praising, hailing, and complimenting are suspicious to me. So I can never be sufficed with Man.

I'm the greatest force Man will ever reckon with. Be wise like a serpent when challenging me. You do so at your own peril, so cherish every moment. Take your best shot when you intellectually attack me, but remember that if you shoot at a king, you better not miss. It's guaranteed that you will revert to the drawing board. But I'm ready for any challenge that lies ahead, even in the offing. Because of my drastic views on Man, you are either with me or against me; you can't be both, in my opinion. If you are against me then something must give in, and I will constantly be a thorn to you and I will reveal to you my difficult side.

I'm beholden, obligated, and indebted to no man; I'm beholden to no man save Jesus Christ. I'm grateful but not bound to any man; I would rather die than to be beholden to a fellow man. I'm owed to no man in this world save Jesus, even the Son of God. How high does Christ, not Man, want me to jump? If I'm wrong, I don't want anyone to give me the benefit of the doubt. If I'm wrong, punish me, fire me, fine me, and cut me no slack; God is my all in all and He will forgive me. I'm not beholden to any man. I'm not seeking impunity from Man.

At this point in my life I either totally serve God hook, line, and sinker, or I partially serve mammon. And to serve mammon is to serve the world. Hence it's God and God only moving forward unto eternal life. It's a point of no return.

Because of the way I observe Man, I uttered a prayer to God saying, "God forgive me for the belittling way I view Your creatures. Father, belittle is an understatement. Father, I know I have committed a sin but You are the Holy One that has bestowed upon me towering wisdom to know all the ways of Man. Forgive me Lord God Almighty but I don't ever want to be like them."

If you don't separate yourself from Man, then Man will decide a fait accompli for you and the rest of the world. I won't be lumped into any category of Man. I'm not content, neither am I sufficient to be a Man; hence, I can never be a race-baiter, even if I pretend to. A pretentious spirit won't last a minute in me because light and darkness don't comprehend.

Wisdom differentiates me from Man. Because of the wisdom God has endowed on me, the only thing clearly human about me is the physical. I can't compare my wisdom to Man; I would be insulting and condemning myself. God Almighty through the Holy Spirit has given me wisdom above every other man's wisdom on earth.

People are puzzled as to why I, without hesitation, turn the other cheek when being offended. If I don't turn the other cheek, it means that Man has overtaken me. It means that I am content to be a Man. It means that I love sin more than I love God. It means that the wisdom of the world has overtaken the wisdom that God has graced upon me.

I differentiate myself from Man. I don't act like another human being. My behavior is classy and flawless. I won't be looked upon as a stereotypical Man. It's incumbent that the first impression someone has on me be vague, and without judgment.

"Saul, Saul why prosecute thou Me? It is hard to kick against the goads,"-Acts 9 verse 5. People claim that I'm stubborn; yes, I'm stubborn, but not unto God but to Man. I savor the things of God and not the things of Man. If I herald and self-proclaim to be the wisest person on earth, then rest assured that I will kick against the goads; I will kick against Man. I will be stubborn to Man. I live by the word of the Potter not the word of the clay. Man has refused to do what is right, so you have to be abjectly stubborn toward Man.

I am not God Almighty so I'm not giving any Man a second chance. I take no prisoners. I don't cut any slack. If you mess up, you have messed up for life. Life has never been fair since when Adam sinned. Yes, I will accept you, but my acceptance comes with a scarlet letter. My mother conceived me in sin so I'm not giving sinners a second chance.

Put me in a room with Rush Limbaugh or any other ultra-conservative; I will be the corrupter while Rush will be the one that has been corrupt. I can't be influenced by Man. I'm above being influenced by Man.

Take caution while dialoging with me because I judge every word that people speak professionally to me. I perceive Man's intentions right from the get-go. I wouldn't let any pronounce utterance that Man utters to me slip through the crack. I won't suffer any word of significance to go undetected.

I'm doing everything to complete my mission on earth. I'm attempting to change the world. I'm not trying to change individual lives. I wouldn't have the patience for that. Someone else has been appointed for that. I'm trying my utmost best to change the world, albeit I know that I'm fighting a losing battle, but not every Man is meant to make it to Heaven. In this day and age are people still trying to change their lives? Changing individual lives means being intimate, and a prophet has no honor in his hometown; I'm here to change the world not to change individual lives.

The only challenge to me in this life is exploring the Almighty God. Satan's temptations and Man's trials don't qualify as challenges to me.

Smallest Minority

I study myself, I scrutinize my ways. I judge my ways, I size myself up. I am aware of everything I do and every word that proceeds out of my mouth. I am very careful when I am praying to God. But with Man I can always turn an offensive comment to a polite comment. Because every word that comes out of the mouth of God sojourned in me, but I won't tempt the Word of God.

I'm a thorn to all of mankind around my way. Woe unto that Man who has laid his eyes on me, because they have been judged. Lucifer, who is synonymous with Satan, remains hell-bent in dragging Man to be with him in Hell Fire. As for me, I'm bound to be a thorn to Man all the days of my life because Man refused to wholeheartedly worship the Most High God. I'm difficult for mankind, just as Satan is evil to mankind. I yearn to ruffle people's feathers; it's a scheme to revert Man to the Word of God. While Satan is drawing Man away from God, on the other hand I and the righteous men of God are drawing Man back to God. It's a tug of war.

The reason why I inevitably have problems with Man is because God didn't create me for mediocrity but for His greatness; hence, I'm the greatest force that Man can ever reckon with on earth. God has sanctified a great anointing upon me like He did to Lucifer, even the son of the morning. God has anointed me with wisdom, knowledge, and understanding—by and large, the seven spirits of God.

Am I handicapped? I never look down at myself. It's inevitable that Man looks down at me, but I look down at Man too because to me mortals are dimwits wisdom-wise. It is not a matter of an eye for an eye, it's a matter of truth.

Let no mortal who believes in God Almighty look down on themselves. Because after God created Man, God looked back and saw that Man was created "good." And I confess to you that no human being dead or alive that has ever been created is more special than me, even Nndy, not even the prophet Moses. If I'm not special then no human being ever created is or was special. From my standpoint, pure wisdom from God is the most valuable gift in this life on earth. What Moses did was impeccable and unparalleled, but at the end of the day, God could have easily chosen someone else to do what Moses did. Someone else could successfully execute the role that Moses played in the Bible. All powers belong to God. For everything that Moses did, it was God that led Moses and held Moses. The only man who is more worthy than me in this life is Jesus Christ, even the Son of the Highest. You can take that to the bank. And I will be the first to kneel down before Jesus my Savior, and I will be the last to stand back up.

"Nndy, why do you act like a stranger?" I have been asked that question time without number. People who are acquainted with me all come to the consensus that I act like I'm a stranger. And if I act like a stranger to my people it is not done purposely but it's innate in me. It's because any time I feel belonging, like I'm earthly, something substantive happens that makes me realized that it's not what God wants me to be. From another standpoint, who is the stranger, me or the world? Are they strangers to me or am I a stranger to them? Or do they make me a stranger by their deeds? From the beginning, God has made me a stranger but I wasn't fully aware of it. From the beginning, I wondered why I felt strange to the world. But as I grew older, I realized certainly that it's due to the sins of Man. It's the sins of the world and the ugly, despicable ways of Man that makes the world a stranger out of me.

A colorblind and an unadulterated conservative are automatically distinguished from the ways of Man. Furthermore, a righteous, real, and true individual is naturally distinguished from the ways of Man. Whether all else fails or not, I don't change who I am. I am real and true in season and out of season.

I don't have the patience for trivial things. People are dying every second; hence, people are dumped into the bottomless pit every second of the day, so I utilize this little time left to preach to those who are chosen to be saved.

I don't comment on trivia. I seldom remark on things that people do. I won't have the patience to talk about some absurd mass murder or rapist, etc. I do comment on what people say that is of substance. Everything to me is trivial and meaningless except the truth about conservatism and the Word of God.

Only grave issues warrant my time. Summon me only when it a small matter of life and death. I have bigger fish to fry than petite domestic issues. I don't have the patience for trifling matters. Summon me when the rubber hits the road; summon me when all else seems to fail.

I'm human physical but not mentally. I have to live a pretentious life, if I have to survive this life on earth. I pretend when I'm doing earthly things because that is the only way I could live this life without being serious. Life is too easy for me to always be serious. What I mean by "pretending" is not pretending as in faking but pretending as in suppressing myself. There is no acting when I'm worshiping God; that is the only time I'm serious.

Apostle Excel is the wisest (of heart) person in the world because he is a person whom God Almighty communicates with on a regular basis. Apostle Excel knows the true meaning of the words in the Bible. I believe certainly that a man who knows the true meaning of the Word of God from Genesis to Revelation has to be the wisest person in this world, bar none.

I saw Rush Limbaugh on the twenty-ninth day of the eleventh month of 2011 in New York City—albeit, not face to face, but a few feet away from his pulpit. And I assure you that there is no man wiser on this planet that Rush Limbaugh. He is the wisest (of mind) person in this world. Rush is God's gift to Man. I disclose a truth to you that when Rush Limbaugh passes away, that will be the end of America. And the fall of America will be great. The only reason other than God Almighty Himself that America remains the greatest county in this world is because of Rush Limbaugh. You could take that to the bank.

The Holy Spirit is undisputedly the wisest Person on earth. It goes without saying, because the wisdom of Jesus Christ is the wisdom of the Holy Spirit, which is also the wisdom of God Almighty.

I beseeched God to perfect the wisdom He has favored unto me. I bid God to make me perfect in worshipping Him with songs. And God has perfected the wisdom He has bestowed unto me, so also He has perfected my worshiping of Him. The third of my requests from God Almighty is pending,—perhaps because the prince of Persia is trying to hold back that request—but at the end of the day, God's Will will prevail for my perfect beauty to manifest.

Because no man is good, I won't be caught dead behaving like man; I won't be caught dead doing what man does. I won't be caught dead living the lifestyle of man, because at the end of the day only God is good. At the end of the day, no man is good. So why would I want to be like man if at the end of the day man is evil? Since God created me as a man, then I won't be caught dead acting like a man. I'm not going to be numbered. Therefore, I have no respect for man; all my respect is for God and God only. But I love man as much as I love myself. I love my helpmate more than I love myself but I will never wish to be like any man ever created. The lion's share of blame happened to be placed on Adam.

You can't let any man overtake you in this life. You can't look up to any man but Jesus Christ. That is why I get raked over the coals because of my stubbornness to man. You can't be subordinate to man but only to God Almighty. You could admire man, you could learn from man—but don't yield to man, yield to God. Don't let man see the end of your wisdom. If you are in the process of being outfoxed, go down swinging; throw a monkey wrench on that person who's on the verge of outfoxing you.

I have no respect for man because no man has forsaken all and followed Jesus Christ. Mark 10:29 says, "And Jesus answered and said, 'Verily I say unto you, there is no man that hath left house, or brethren, or sisters, or father, or mother, or wife, or children, or lands, for my sake, and the gospel's.'" I have no respect for man because no Man is good; no not even one Man is good.

You could endeavor all your life to be a good, true, and nice man—but remember that at the end of the day, the only true story is the story of Jesus. At the end of the day, man will always have skepticism and criticism against you. The only one who is good is God Himself. The last time I checked, the apostle Peter denied Christ on three back-to-back occasions. If I'm not mistaken, wasn't the apostle Paul in dissention with the apostle Peter? The last time I checked, Moses killed any Egyptian in cold blood. Thus saith the Lord, "Thou shalt not murder," but the prophet Samuel beheaded King Agag. Thus saith the Lord, "Thou shalt not commit adultery," but King David was an adulterer. I thought father Abraham impregnated his maidservant? John the Baptist asked, "Do we look for another?" thereby doubting and having second thoughts if Jesus was the Son of God. For crying out loud, this was the man who just baptized Jesus Christ and confessed that He was the Messiah. No man is good, no not one. Even Jesus, who was sinless and who died for the sins of man, recused Himself of the notion of being good.

I live my life the right way for the sake of my loved ones; God will spare them because they are my people. Like Abraham and Lot where Abraham intercedes for Lot. So it's incumbent upon me to do what is right all the days of my life because God elected me to bear the responsibility of all my loved ones, even thousands of them. Living the right way in life is interceding for my people on earth. I will take the arrow should I detour from the Word of God. I remember like it was yesterday when an acquaintance said, "Nndy, I don't have to go to the tabernacle because you are going for me." He then proceeded to compare my intercession with Christ taking away Man's sin. Living the right way of life amends my loved ones' transgressions; it's an act of interceding and atoning for their and my iniquities.

I get blamed for everything; my people take out their frustration, unanswered prayer requests, shortcomings, etc. on me—as if I'm the one that caused their dire, unfavorable, and abject situation. If the righteous men are going to judge the angels on Judgment Day, you could take it to the bank that none of my people that believe in God will be condemned, because I make it incumbent to live a righteous life every given day. As Moses was the prophet of God and as Paul was an apostle of Christ, so also is Nndy a servant of the Holy Spirit.

Prophet of the Holy Spirit

The joy of making it to Heaven has passed, but the joy of the Word of God and the joy of worshiping God Almighty every day of my life is ever before me. I can't get enough of that joy and I'm utterly gratified to God for molding me to love worshiping Him. That joy is an eternal joy; hence, it will never pass away. Worshiping God is the best thing in life on earth, bar none. You can take that to the bank.

God has given me three perfections. One is the wisdom He has favored me with, which is made perfect by the Holy Spirit; the second is the perfection of worshiping Him through Jesus Christ; and the last perfection is the beauty of my missing rib in Iifi.

I'm a prophet of the Holy Spirit. I can't be appointed by Man to be a man of the cloth because the Holy Spirit has already elected me as His prophet. And as such I'm only subjected to the Holy Spirit on earth. God anointed me with a paramount anointing like the anointing He bestowed on Lucifer.

God has given me an excellent spirit. I'm in a league of my own in terms of my worship of God in Heaven. I have my own rules and regulations that if it should be revealed to Man, he would conclude that I am crazy and demented. And I break my rules on some occasions. I have to walk on eggshells while carrying out my rules. I'm not subjected to Man in my worshiping of God and there is no contentment in my worship of God.

I'm doing everything to complete my mission on earth, so when I am on a mission, the mission is obviously in the forefront of my mind; the mission is the be-all and the end-all. And I must do everything to complete my mission. Until I get to the destination, the dead will bury their dead. There won't be any detour from the destination of my mission, even an issue of life and death. So before I embark on a mission, I must make sure that every man will be ignored, save the Word of God.

I live a godly life which implies that my life is not lived in vain. I refuse to let the things I do to be in vain. I refuse to love the pleasure of sin. I withhold myself from breaking bread with the corrupt Man. Since I live a godly life for the most part of my life, most of the earthly things I do, I do as if I'm doing it in a spiritual way. I take a spiritual approach in doing earthly things. Nothing Man or Mother Nature does stuns me; wonders have ended for me.

Jesus Christ sacrificing His life for mankind wasn't in vain. So Man will suffer the consequences of Jesus' death through the second death if they don't accept and believe in Him.

I don't want to be regenerated to the Heaven that once housed Lucifer who disconcerted the Almighty God in Heaven. I want to be regenerated to a Heaven in which sin never reared its ugly head. I want to be regenerated to a Heaven that is as holy as God. God is too holy to still suffer that very Heaven that once housed Lucifer to exist. I love God more than I love Heaven. Because if I love Heaven as much as I love God, it means that I love the sin that Lucifer committed in Heaven too. "Behold, Heaven and earth shall pass away but my words shall not pass away-" Matthew 24 verse 35. I don't contest to be in the Heaven that will pass away; I contest to be in the Word of God that will live forever.

Millions of people just want to make it to the Kingdom of Heaven but we should strive to be an Elijah or a Moses before God, not just one of the children of Israel who were saved. Being regenerated to Heaven is not a day's job. It's the whole lifetime span of a Man. Heaven is real. Sometimes I dread and am scared of Judgment Day, but once I think of the mother of the sons Zebedee and Christ's ultimate sacrifice, I feel renewed. So what about the mother of the sons of Zebedee? I don't merely want to make it to Heaven; I want to sit next to God on His Throne.

The mother of the sons of Zebedee didn't ask Christ for her sons to just make it to Heaven, she asked for her two sons to sit next to either side of Christ's throne in Heaven. In order words, making it to Heaven wasn't even a question for the mother of the sons of Zebedee; that was a fait accompli. Her major concern was for her sons, Apostle John and Apostle James, to be prominent in God's kingdom. If God should appoint me to be the one who judges who is regenerated to Heaven, then only a hatful will be regenerated; even myself, I would be in danger of not being regenerated. Only the Holy God Almighty is worthy to be in Heaven alone.

From the beginning, God's chosen people were the children of Israel, even the children of Jacob. Relatives to me are those whom God has made me love. And I love them; they are the children of Israel to me.

Family and friends, through and through conservatives, and true Christians, are those who I refer to as my relatives. I love ultra conservatives like Rush Limbaugh, Sean Hannity, Tom DeLay, Rick Santorum, Sarah Palin, and Michelle Malkin; I would die for them all. They are the pillars of conservatism. You can't repent from the sin of blaspheming against God the Holy Spirit, even if you attempt to, because Christ said such sin cannot be forgiven. So if I'm an unrepentant conservative, then I'm a blasphemer against the Holy Ghost conservative. I don't love fellow conservatives because I yearn for them to love me back; my love for them is not meant to be reciprocal. I love them because I want them to be regenerated to God's kingdom. They know the truth, and the truth has set them free.

I will throw myself under the bus for my family and friends. But I have nothing much to say about my family and friends because a prophet is without honor in his hometown.

I would die for my relatives but I won't desire to be like any of them because I won't be accused by Lucifer of being a smoker, a fornicator, a thief, or any other vice. I would never wish to be like another human being.

I love my loved ones because I want them to make it to Heaven. My love for my people is not meant to be reciprocal but as Jesus loved Peter. Christ didn't love Peter for Peter to love Christ back. If I choose to love someone then I have chosen to ignore a betraying or backstabbing that I may encounter. Any unbecoming and injurious act from someone who I chose to love has become part of that love I profess to have for them. Reciprocal love is not what I crave. There is no Man in this world who I love for the sake of them to love me in return. Therefore, betrayal, denial, character assassinations, etc., by them will not be condemned because my love for them is not meant to be reciprocal. My loved ones have been passed to salvation and no matter what they do to me, I would never visit their offense. They can't do any harm to me verbally or non-verbally that will make me change on them. I have a "what would Christ do" love for them.

Strangers and the people of the world to me are similar to the Philistines, the Moabites, and the Amalekites, etc., who were the children of Israel's enemies; they were rejected by God Almighty. They have no part in me; hence, they are considered walking dead and I don't sympathize with their grief, neither will I wear sackcloth and ashes for their misfortune. I'm not known for pretending so I will save my crocodile tears for the people of the world. God will not suffer any of my relative to die like the people of the world.

I thank the Potter every day of my life. I would without doubt have surely hated my life if God didn't embed me with His wisdom and understanding; I would perhaps have killed myself. The last thing I want in this life is to be like the average man.

Nothing in this world is mine except the beauty of my missing rib, the wisdom from the Holy Spirit, and the worship of God. I'm the greatest force that any man would ever reckon with.

There is nothing better in this world than worshiping God. The joy, bliss, and ecstasy that I get from worshiping God with hymns and songs of praise is indescribable.

God has graced me with the wisdom to know all the ways of Man; hence, God has enabled me to see the end of Man's wisdom on earth. I'm on a pinnacle of the temple, but unlike Jesus, I might heed to Satan's request because I'm only but a mortal and there is nothing left to learn from Man but the Word of God.

Perfect beauty has to settle for the third most important thing in my life. I died and went to heaven after I had that perfect dream about Iifi on the seventeenth day of the third month of 2013. But how will I feel when the perfect dream and my supplication to God Almighty manifests?

And I tell you that if God didn't designate me to be the wisest in this generation, He wouldn't have hastened to bring me back to America, even to New York City, which is the greatest city in the world. He would not have installed in me an utmost love for my missing rib in London—so much so, that her name means wisdom, if being interpreted to English.

I came to a point in my life where I only listen to the true Gospel of God and Rush Limbaugh conservatism. I came to a point in my life where everything people say is idle tale and I will be in idle time listening to them, whether in person or on television. But I'm not rude to people, so I must stomach their idle talk. I worship God with songs every day of my life with intent. I get so agitated with myself when I'm disturbed while worshiping God.

God declared the end from the beginning; God saw the end of the world the same day He created the heavens and the earth. God saw and declared the end from the beginning; therefore, daily communicating with God is making and seeing the future with God. God saw the end from the beginning; hence, our lives on earth have already been lived. We are living a life that has already been lived in the eyes of God. I refer you to Ecclesiastes 3:15.

I pray for the forgiveness of my unborn children's sins because I can only see from today until the day I die on earth. If I live for the next thirty-three years on earth, then I can, even from today, see the sixty-sixth year of my life on earth. My unborn children are already born in God's eyes; they are already living their lives in God's eyes. In other words, when Christ came and died for the world, I was already, in God's eyes living this life that I'm living.

Last Vestige of Truth

I'm obsessed with the truth; I am obsessed with the Word of God. No man is more righteous than me in the radioactive issues of abortion and homosexual marriage because I cut no slack and I take no prisoners. It's my job on earth to tackle the pleasures of sin— tackle the pleasures of Satan, if you will. I possess a bully pulpit on radioactive issues like fornication and homosexuality, etc., because it happens to be at the top of Satan's pecking order. What the world loves is what I condemn. As time goes on, Man will change the Bible and eradicate the words that condemn homosexual marriage. They are gradually changing the King James Version of the Bible.

If you sow fornication you would surely reap a misbegotten child, a bastard if you will.

I have never been an ordinary person, neither am I a big fish in a small pond, so I wouldn't be reduced to silence over judging Man's immoral ways. I wouldn't be censored or subdued in voicing out Man's egregious, corrupt ways. God didn't make me mediocre; God made me with greatness. The common people and the average Joes are scared to judge the truth. Children born out of wedlock are illegitimate children from unwed parents; they are born out of disobedience from the Word of God. They are children of fornication; but babies born to married couples are born out of righteousness.

I believe in an abstinence lifestyle for the unmarried. In the first place, should you commit adultery and fornication, you have committed a grave sin against God. There are more questions than answers in such a pleasurable act. I'm not condemning the intense thought of fornication; I'm only but condemning the act of fornication itself. Christ warned that just looking with lust at a woman is a sin of fornication and one has already committed fornication in their hearts. Christ was talking about the thought of fornication.

There are heaps of problems awaiting you on the horizon if you live a promiscuous life and if you commit these acts. It's common sense. What are the gains in fornicating and living in sin? They are more misery than pleasure. Every sin we commit, especially sin involving another human, there will be consequences and repercussions. The price must be paid. The day of vengeance and reckoning won't be palatable.

I'm very controversial; I'm a lone wolf. Radioactive issues are what I strive for; they are what I feed on. I chomp at the bit to condemn cases involving those issues. Why do I love to tug on one's heart string? I don't shy away from what people avoid with a ten-foot pole. Yet I don't put my mouth where every conversation lies; I keep my own counsel. I'm not giving credence to remarks. If I do converse, I converse solely on controversial issues. Issues that people don't want to hear. Nobody wants to hear the unadulterated truth. There is no point in having a conversation with people on what they want to hear.

Abraham interceded for Lot to save Lot from the destruction of Sodom and Gomorrah. I tell you that America has become Sodom and Gomorrah times eleven. So if America becomes Noah's ship and only eight people survive the Great Flood, I bet you that Rush Limbaugh will be among the surviving eight. True conservatives and Christians will be among the surviving eight. Gay marriage supporters and advocates and those without opinions on homosexual marriage will perish, and only then will I be sufficient. It's not too late to revert to the Word of God. But certain people will inescapably turn back like Lot's wife; hence, they will become salt.

I'm against prostitution—hook, line, and sinker. At the deepest depth, at the eleventh hour, at the very end of the day, I'm not against the vessel that is being used for prostitution—I'm against the act itself. I'm against the sin that is committed. So when I assert that I'm judging a woman who is a prostitute, when you dig deep you realize that I'm only judging the act being committed. But it must appear as if I'm judging the woman herself because I have to compel the harlot to be contrite for her acts.

You have to be able to read between the lines and read the stitches on the fast ball to understand that all I'm doing is defending the sinner but denouncing and condemning the sin. By and large, at the last minute of the eleventh hour I wasn't judging the actor but I was judging the action. Let God be the One to cut any given fornicator or idolizer some slack. Certain people have called me evil because I don't budge on my extreme stance against abortion and prostitution. Who is more evil—someone who is totally against abortion and prostitution or someone who sees nothing wrong with abortion and prostitution. God condemns fornication and whoredom and if we are God's children then we will hold that tenet to the hilt without bias—but we want to cut people slack.

I'm lock, stock, and barrel against abortion—in any way, shape, or form—because I'm not content to be Man, thereby I'm not accepting his immoral ways. I give no room for sympathy. Whether the abortion is due to rape, incense, or what have you, I don't care so long as a potential child is in danger of being prematurely killed. I don't have any sympathy in my heart for those who beg to have an abortion. I'm doing two things here: I'm interceding for the innocent fetus that is on the verge of being killed and I'm doing my utmost from admonishing the culprit (an abortion-bound woman) from committing a grave sin. Yes, sin is sin but I tell you that the blood of that potential child will be upon your head on earth and during the Day of Judgment. I don't take any prisoners, whether family or friends. So my judgment on the woman committing abortion starts immediately.

Living and trying to live a righteous life is constantly in the forefront of my mind. I'm much more righteous in my actions than in my words. God looks at the heart of Man; the words of Man are predominately lip service. Having the mindset to do the right thing all the time is part and parcel of my life, and because I was conceived in sin, when I'm wrong, I am only wrong in innocence. In other words, I'm only wrong without intentions—unless I want to be wrong just to upset the opposition, like purposely being wrong to those of a different ideology.

Homosexuality gives fornication and adultery credence because homosexual marriage is not merely a sin but it's an abomination of the worst possible degree. Having said that, one will rather support heterosexuality done in sin than homosexuality? One will have to support and condone fornication in order to destroy homosexuality? In this situation, you can't have it both ways. You can't be against fornication and also against homosexuality. Because fornication, although it is a grave sin, it's not an abomination. Homosexuality gives fornication and adultery credence. Would a God-fearing servant rather suffer unwed couples to be together or would they rather suffer homosexual couples to be together? So at the end of the day, fornication will be upheld while homosexuality will be condemned.

God never sinned. Jesus never sinned so Jesus doesn't know the lust associated in fornication and adultery. Jesus doesn't physically know the difficulty in overcoming fornication and adultery, because when He came to earth He lived a sinless life. God says Man should not commit adultery, etc., but it's easy to say. And it's impossible for God to physically know the difficulties in overcoming the temptation of fornication, etc., because God can never assume Himself as a Man; if He does so, then He will cease from being God. By and large, God can only use a vessel (a man) to ascertain the difficulties in overcoming fornication, etc. And by and large, the only way a sinful man can overcome the intense desire of fornication is by God's intervention; it's only if God prevents Man from sinning, like He did to Abimelech in regards to Sarah (Abraham's wife.) Because of sin, Christ was not conceived by the mating of sinners but Christ was conceived through an immaculate conception by the Holy Spirit via the Virgin Mary. Christ didn't have any offspring because if He did, he would be involved with sin.

John 8 verse 32 "Ye know the truth and the truth shall set you free." There are pinnacles of truth; truth has degrees. You have to believe in the truth in order for the truth to set you free. To what degree do you believe in the truth? To what extent? How much faith do you have in the truth? Knowing the truth is one thing but it's another thing to believe in the truth. The truth will set you free, but how free are you? How much of the Word of God is in you? You have to believe in the truth in order for it to set you free. How much truth are they in John 14:12 says, "Verily, verily, I say unto you, he that believeth on me, the works that I do shall he do also; and greater works than these shall he do, because I go unto my Father?" And how much truth are they in Mark 10:18 says, "And Jesus said unto him, 'Why callest thou me good? There is none good but one, that is, God?'" Even those in whom the truth abides can't stand the truth; they can't swallow the truth, because truth surpasses truth. Christ said, "I am the way, the truth, and the life; no man cometh unto the Father, but by me." (John 14:6)—that is the truth. Matthew 24 verse 35, Jesus said, "Heaven shall pass away but my word will never pass away"—that is the truth too, but truth surpasses truth. The truth in Matthew 24 surpasses the truth in John 14.

Forerunner of the Second Coming

And it came to pass that after those days, Apostle Dave, a great man of God from Virginia and a comrade of Apostle Excel, was sent by the Lord to reveal God's plan for me. Before Apostle Dave prayed for me, he said that I will "walk on water." And revealed further in his prayer for me that I will "raise the dead," etc.

Do you want Jesus to heed Satan's advice? Do you want Jesus to turn stone into bread?

I want Jesus Christ to turn stone into bread because the Gentiles are not worshiping God the way they ought to. I want Jesus to turn stone into bread because the Gentiles are supporting gay marriages in their churches and even in the pulpit. I want Jesus to turn stone into bread because the Gentiles are blaspheming the son of the Highest, even the Almighty. The stones that Satan tempted Jesus to turn to bread are not ordinary stones. Apostle Excel revealed that the stones that Satan was referring to are the Gentiles. And who are the Gentiles? The Gentiles are the Christians. Satan didn't want salvation for the Gentiles so he urged Jesus to turn stone to bread so that the bread (Gentiles) will be consumed.

I will be the first to cast a stone at any given fornicator or any given adulterer or any given malefactor. You have been judged. And let not any man follow me and cast stones at a culprit lest the next stone that will be cast will be on that man (the imitator.) You don't know for what reason I am casting stones at a culprit, so don't cast stones with me.

In John chapter 8 verse 7, Christ made the statement, "He that is without sin among you, let him first cast a stone at her" *before* He willingly gave His life for us, not *after* He gave His life for the remission of our sins. So I won't hesitate to cast the first stone on any given rapist, idolizer, or any given prostitute, because Christ died to take away my sins.

The truth is the truth. I'm the last vestige of truth. I am glad that God made me a colorblind conservative. I loathe Man's egregious attitudes. Hence, in passing, I preached vehemently against his attitude. I am a cherub; therefore, I abhor the ways of the generic man. So if Men pick up stones to stone me, I wouldn't know what their bone and grief against me are, nor would I know for what they want to stone me? What you don't know will not hurt you. What is the common denominator? You have the liberals, the gay activists, the abortionists, African American rabble-rousers, single unmarried mother crusaders, single unmarried deadbeat fathers, feminists, Christians in name only, convenient conservatives, false men of the cloth, etc.—all gathering stones to stone me but they can't agree on a common ground why they want to stone me. They are confounded.

An eye for an eye is human nature. It's not human nature for you to turn the other cheek. It's not a knee-jerk reaction to turn the other cheek; rather, it's the Gospel for you to turn the other cheek. So a true servant of God should suffer the turning of the other cheek to be human nature. An eye for an eye shouldn't be human nature or part of life. I'm an arbitrator on what should or what shouldn't be human nature. I'm running against human nature; I defile human nature. If you slap me on one cheek, you must slap me on the other cheek. An eye for an eye is the end of human nature.

With all the wisdom God has endowed me, it's almost impossible for Satan to tempt me without me perceiving and anticipating it. I behold most of Satan's temptation coming a mile away; hence, by the time it reaches me it is void. Sometimes I observe what is not happening. I tempt Satan in order for him tempt me. I purposely put myself in his path. Satan knows what I like; he knows what entices me, so I put myself out there purposely. Sometimes I purposely make myself angry so as to tempt Satan to tempt me. I refuse to suffer Satan to have the last laugh.

God uses people to test you, so you have to be alert and take caution while approaching. Take, for instance, Satan and King David. God caused Satan to tempt David to number the people of Israel. After David heeded Satan's temptation, God turned around and punished David for numbering the people of Israel because His anger was kindled against David and Israel as a whole. Satan, even that old serpent, is a great servant of God and he will always be an agent of God Almighty. I refer you to 2 Samuel 24:1 juxtaposed with 1 Chronicles 21:1.

I tempt myself before Satan tempts me. I know what I admire and Satan also is aware of what I admire. But my admiration is progressive; it's changeable. What I fancy today, I could detest tomorrow, and what I detest yesterday, I could fancy again today. So I go before Satan's temptation and since I know that Satan knows what I'm fond of, I go before Satan's temptation. I tempt myself before Satan attempts to tempt me.

After fasting forty days and forty nights, wouldn't the last place to go be the wilderness? So who tempted who? Jesus provoked Satan to tempt Him. The Spirit of God that led Christ to the wilderness to fast for forty days and forty nights by and large tempted Satan to tempt Jesus, and Satan couldn't let the opportunity to tempt Jesus go begging. If Christ would have gone to the tabernacle while fasting, then Satan wouldn't have tempted Christ in that instance. But Christ went to the wilderness; Christ beard the lion in his den.

What was Christ doing in the wilderness while He fasted for forty days and forty nights? Christ provoked Satan to tempt him. So who tempted who? Christ, for all intents and purposes, tempted Satan to tempt Him because if Christ didn't long for Satan to tempt Him, He wouldn't have gone to the wilderness. But because Christ so much loved the Gentiles, because He came to save the Gentiles, Christ knew that by going to the wilderness, Satan lay in wait to tempt Him. But note that it was the Spirit of God that led Christ to the wilderness. So Satan is a servant of God; he did his job by tempting the Son of God—albeit Satan didn't get the result he longed for.

Doubled-Edged Sword

The Lord has bestowed upon me the seven spirits of God, and the spirit of judgment happens to be one of the spirits. Because of my God-given wisdom, it's impossible for me to live this life without judging people.

God is good because if God should appoint me to judge Man, only a minimal percent of the world would be saved. I'm heartless toward those who refuse to heed to the Word of God.

I would shoot first and I wouldn't ask questions later; asking questions is irrelevant. If you are innocent then you will be redeemed. But because you are a stranger to the Word of God, you have already been judged. Your sin has judged you.

I'm not judging Man; in the grand scheme of things, its Man's heinous and egregious actions, attitudes, and lifestyles that have judged him. Your reprehensible and abominable actions, attitudes, and lifestyles have testified against you. Your sins have been judge. Man is judged at first sight. I judge Man's attitude and Man's action at first sight. I judge Man's language and utterance at first hearing. Man is judged right from the outset.

I'm judging people but I am not rendering a sentence. My judgment doesn't culminate in condemnation, it culminates in the plea for repentance. And if I plead for God's forgiveness on Man's behalf, rest assured that I wouldn't treat you with kid gloves. My judgment doesn't finish the sentence; it's only God's judgment that finishes the sentence.

No matter what my relatives (family, friends, true conservatives, and Christians) do, love will always trump judgment;

love will always go before judgment. But that is the sin in me. If Iifi or Linda and Hetty (my sisters) do something utterly unbecoming, I'm not going to judge them in open but in my heart I will entreat for them. Under no circumstances, come hell or high water, will I ever condemn them. I would never denounce my relatives; I will never judge them. When I see my relatives, I see love first. And that love that I see prevents me from judging them. And that Love is Jesus. When I hear the words of arch conservatives, like Sean Hannity, Rush Limbaugh, or Mark Levin, I hear the truth first; hence, the truth prevents me from judging them. That Truth is the Holy Spirit.

Strangers will always be judged; I wouldn't even suffer them to finish their sentence before I judge them. The words will still be in their mouth and I would instantly judge them. And even if what they utter was fair, the fact that they are strangers will judge them. Satan could also be fair. We have nothing in common and I have nothing to say to strangers but the Word of God.

There is a double standard between judging my relatives and judging strangers, but life has never been fair. It's not a matter of bias blinding the eye. Besides, Jesus said that He came to bring the sword; He came to divide. "Think not that I am come to send peace on earth: I came not to send peace, but a sword"-Matthew 10 verse 34. Again Jesus didn't come to save the whole world; Christ came to save those whom God apportioned for Him. "I pray for them; I pray not for the world, but for them which thou hast given me, for they are thine"— John 17 verse 9.

I judge sin, not sinners, but my judging is subliminal; hence, I'm accused of judging Man himself. How can I judge Man when that will be done on Judgment Day? Don't I first have to see the end of time before I conduct a dress rehearsal for Judgment Day? Man never ceases to accuse me of attempting to be God. But I tell you that there are many dry runs in the Holy Bible that depict and forerun that dreadful Day of Judgment.

I wouldn't condemn any Man whom God created. If I condemn Man, that means that I have condemned God's work. That means that I'm judging God's work. But I'm judging sin and sin is not God's work; sin is Satan's work. And Satan is my only adversary in this life.

I reveal to you this unearthed wisdom not to always hearken to man's utterance. Anyone who judges man is always tarred and feathered. It has always been said not to judge people, but if you don't judge man, how do you expect to be a saint of God? If you don't judge man on earth how do you expect to judge angels? First Corinthians 6:2-3 says, "Do ye not know that the saints shall judge the world? And if the world shall be judged by you, are ye unworthy to judge the smallest matters? Know ye not that we shall judge angels? How much more things that pertain to this life?"

The judging of a fellow man is not wrong, so long as the judgment is done righteously. If you don't righteously judge man, then you won't be qualified to judge angels; hence, you won't be qualified to be a saint of God, and by and large you won't be regenerated to the Kingdom of God. So judging man righteously is a forerunner and a dry run to the judging of angels on the last day.

Who will cast the first stone? Christ has already died and resurrected and He intercedes for my sins to be forgiven, so I will cast the first stone at any given prostitute. I will cast the first stone at any character who blasphemes against the Godhead. And I will cast the first stone at a murderer, a rapist, and a witch. Having said that, my casting of stones is not unto death, rather it is unto correction. It's not unto condemning for sentencing but is unto condemning for recognition of sins. By and large, it's condemning unto warning.

I'm judging Man but I am not sentencing Man; I'm judging Man but I am not condemning Man. I'm condemning the sin, not condemning the sinner. I am sentencing the sin but I am not sentencing the sinner. Only the Lord God Almighty sentences sinners unto eternal condemnation, unto the second death. And the good Lord will do so on Judgment Day—the Day of Reckoning, if you will.

My words are a double-edged sword. They preach to me and to the reader. They are an acid test to me and to the reader.

In closing, I view all human beings as little kids running around playing: getting concerned where it's not needed, getting angry over nothing, crying over spilt milk, and fighting and arguing over trivial matters. I can't associate with human beings; they are just too immature to be devoutly involved with.

I don't hate any human being ever. I judge human beings as innocent babies that once in a while get into trouble. I don't hate any human being whom God created; I just hate the sin not the sinner. The sin that I hate in Man is the language of Man, the ideology of Man, and the attitude of Man, etc. The Almighty God in Heaven, the King of all Days, and the precious Holy Ghost have not given me the heart of hatred.

Half of my mission on earth is completed. My throne is built above the throne of any man on earth. My wisdom is perfect but since there is no end to sin, there is no end to the wisdom God has bestowed upon me. Sin has to be countered.

No material thing in this world is mine. I refuse to reap where I didn't sow and I'm not going to stake my claim from the end when I wasn't there from the beginning. Hence, only three things in this world are mine. My worship of God is the first most important thing in this world that is mine. And when I'm at a climax in worshiping God in spirit and in truth, the joy in the spiritual realm exceeds nothing that I have ever experience before.

My wisdom from God the Holy Spirit, which has enabled me to write four books, and which allows me to learn from Rush Limbaugh and Apostle Excel, is mine. God Almighty hastily made me aware of all the ways of Man so that I would have nothing else to study, save the Word of God. I love God the Most High so much that I will die for Him as Jesus died for me. I serve God and God only. I have no other alternative; I have no other option. God has to forsake me; I can't forsake God.

I have no respect for Man because I reverence God to the hilt. I worship God to the most possible extreme, so there is no way I could have respect for Man. I have an immeasurable reverence for God to the hilt, so much so that there is no room for respect for Man.

Since God is righteously unfair in regard to who is regenerated to Heaven, I have to claim to be the wisest person on earth. I want God Almighty to confess that He has made me the wisest person on earth. Only then will my life on earth be justified and validated.

My beauty is my missing rib, Iifi. Remember that Lucifer, that great dragon from the beginning, took away one of my eyes. Regardless of the damage done to the right side of my face, it is still beautifying.

The joy of making Heaven has passed away but the joy of worshiping Jesus Christ with songs of life every day of my life on earth will never pass away.

I don't hate any mortal in this world. I hate the sin but love the sinners. I don't give any cushion, I don't cut any slack, I don't take any prisoners, and I don't give second chances. It's okay to be someone with a scarlet letter.

I'm not content with the wisdom of this world. Just as Jesus Christ my personal Lord and Savior told Judas Iscariot, I'm telling the whole world, I am telling human beings: "You know what you want to do to me, do it fast."

Nndy and Iifi Journal

Iifi, the Perfection of Beauty

The first time I adored Iifi was in Calabar, Nigeria when we were teenagers; it was a love at first sight experience. I didn't need a second invitation. Albeit we were only young teens, but age is nothing but a number. The first experience with Iifi is engraved in my memory.

The second time I loved Iifi again was short-lived because I was on the verge of leaving Nigeria to America. I was inundated with distractions. Would to God that I never left Nigeria to America; Iifi and I would have been long established, a fait accompli. Age nineteen was the last time I beheld Iifi.

Mercy (Jesus) said no when sin (Satan) tried to take away Iifi's precious life in a car accident; Mercy (Jesus) said no to justice (Satan) when Iifi was face to face with death.

I knew that Iifi was meant to be my future wife when I heard that she died. I just couldn't stomach the horrible news and I just couldn't console myself. Before that horrible news, Iifi was a fading picture, a forgotten figure, and I only seriously thought of her when I was being reminded by my peers across the Atlantic. But that bad tiding resurrected my strong feelings for her and from then onward it slowly became a no retreat, no surrender mission. A mission that might seem impossible will surely be possible with God.

But God be thanked because the tidings of Iifi passing away later turned out to be a rumor. I asked why was a rumor made about her death and why was I chosen to be told? I was overwhelmingly ecstatic to learn that it was a rumor, but why was it out there in the first place? As long as I believe in God, I believe everything happens for a reason. And the reasons are His.

Iifi's story began when she was born in the United Kingdom of Great Britain, even in England. Upon finishing college, Iifi made the grade the first time asking. And her young career is destined to blossom. She is expected to reach a major height, like none of her kindred has ever reached. Iifi has set the benchmark, a clinic for others. Iifi has an enviable job in Central London.

From my childhood I had for some unexplainable reason always loved England even more than I loved my birth county of America and my family's country of Nigeria. And I long assumed myself as an English fellow, and to boot I lived an English lifestyle. And to ascertain that Iifi was born in England, it implies that England to me is the greatest earthly paradise. I will admit that America is the greatest country in the world bar none, but peace trumps greatness. In America no one is exempt from being in danger of being shot. But in England, guns are prohibited. Even the cops, for crying out loud, don't carry firearms. But the cops in New York can't wait to unload and reload their pistol. England has been blessed before America.

England is original. America's existence is due to the Revolutionary War. So America stems from the United Kingdom. As a kid I have always fancied England more than America. I didn't for the life of me know why that was the case. But I ascertained later in life that the reason why it was so was because my missing rib, Iifi, was born in England.

Iifi and I are the third-born of our parents. Iifi and I were both born in foreign lands. And we moved to our parent's country for discipline's sake. And then we returned to our respective countries of birth. And I have known her since when I was thirteen. Iifi and I are meant to be together because husband and wife always look alike—not only in resemblance but in behavior, etc. We both happen to be colorblind. Iifi is colorblind and it makes me so proud that she doesn't see color. It justifies my love for her because God also made me colorblind.

Lucifer was the angel of light; he was the most beautiful of all angels that God created. Archangel Lucifer's beauty is a forerunner of Iifi's beauty. Iifi's beauty is a bright and morning star,—an unadulterated beauty, if you will.

Beauty is in the eyes of the beholder; having said that, everybody who has beheld Iifi confessed that Iifi is nothing less than beautiful and gorgeous. Whether in Europe, Africa, or America, they all sing from the same hymn book.

Iifi's beauty is second to none on earth. Iifi's beauty eclipses the beauty of that beautiful angel of light, Lucifer. There is no ugliness in Iifi's beauty. Obviously because of my blind eye, the right side of my face has surrendered its beauty. But Iifi's beauty complements the blemish on the right side of my face; Iifi's beauty complements my ugliness.

While I was growing up in Nigeria, I had this perfect picture of the type of woman I would one day love to wed. I had this American way that I imagined the character and credentials of whom I would love to be my future wife. And en route to America from Nigeria in 1999, that picture got clearer. And Iifi fit the bill perfectly. I'm determined to make the pipe dream a reality—to turn the pipe dream of the characteristics of the woman that will bear my child into becoming a reality.

The Word of God first mentioned the phase "helpmeet," when God saw that Adam was lonely. Thus God took one of Adam's "ribs" and created a woman who was later called "Eve." Hence, Eve was Adam's missing rib. And right before sin reared its ugly head—that is, right before sin entered into the serpent—Adam took the woman as his "wife."

Christ set the benchmark. I patiently waited until 33 years of age before I ventured into the process of marriage because that was the number of years Jesus my personal Lord and Savior spent on earth.

Iifi is my last friend on earth. I don't desire to have any more friends in my life. The Holy Spirit has filled the vacuum. And the filling is eternal. All of my friends and acquaintances are of yesteryear and as such they are surplus to requirements. Iifi is my last friend on earth. It is not a coincidence that God has made me a person of utmost wisdom and Iifi's name means wisdom. I interpreted that as evidence that Iifi is meant to be my future.

I prayed to the Lord to protect Iifi's every breath and to promote the angels that have been assigned to protect Iifi day and night.

A Virgin Mary Forerunner

Iifi is the beautiful love of my life. The Virgin Mary is a forerunner to Iifi. For as long as I have known Iifi I have never heard any immoral news about Iifi. Save for Iifi, all the other daughters that I have admired in Africa, Europe, and in America, I have been told of their moral failings. For those reasons, I'm not holding my breath to wed a virgin, but what you don't know will not hurt you. It puts a

131

bad taste in my mouth should I think of the aforementioned as wife material—unlike Iifi, who has never been defiled, never been damaged goods. Iifi is a woman of virtue.

If you are a fornicator and lived a promiscuous lifestyle, then what is the purpose of getting married? How godly will that marriage be? You have mocked God should you beseech God to give you a good wife after you lived half of your life in sin. And the reason why I live an abstinent lifestyle is not because of my choice, but it's because God has prevented me from falling in the fornicating, adulterous category. I recognize that I and Iifi are God's reserved.

Iifi is the perfected daughter of God. To me, Iifi is a virgin because God has not suffered me to hear any immoral news about her since when I have loved her. Everything happened for a reason; God saw the end from the beginning. Hence, God knew that this day would come after fourteen years that I will be seeking His face daily petitioning, begging, praying, fasting, worshiping, salivating, and chomping at the bit for Him to give me His daughter for marriage.

Taking a page from Luke 1 verse 35, I beseeched the Holy Spirit to come upon Iifi as she sleeps every night so that she will conceive marital and everlasting love for me; just as the Holy Spirit came upon the Virgin Mary and the power of the Highest was upon the Virgin Mary to conceive Jesus my Lord and my Savior. Christ Jesus died for me and Iifi to be saved, and part of Christ's death was for me and Iifi to be married.

The author and finisher of our faith is Jesus. God spoke faith out of Himself when He created the world. When God said, "Let there be light and there was light," the light was in God. God spoke faith out of Himself and said, "Let there be light and there was light." So if I believe in God, if I have faith in God, then I have faith in the God that spoke faith out of Himself, and what He spoke manifested. So if I say, "Let Iifi be my wife," then she will be my wife because I'm speaking the faith that I have in God that is in God to myself. You speak faith in what you truly believe is within you. Having faith in God means that I'm part of God's faith that He spoke out of Himself from the foundation of the world. I have faith in the God that spoke faith out of Himself and the world was graciously created. Since Jesus is the author and most importatly the finisher of my faith and since I

have the unwaveing faith in God that He has earmarked Iifi for me,
Jesus would have to diminish my faith if Iifi and I are not a couple.

God's Will

If God only does what is His will then there is no need to
plead to Him for what is not in His will because God already knows
what we want—even though what we desire may not be His will.

If God only manifests what is in His will for us, then there
wouldn't be any reason to ask God for our wishes and desires—
especially if we are not sure if what we yearn and request for is in His
will or not. Because at the end of the day, God will only do what is in
His will—i.e., the perfect will of God. But there is also the permissive
will of God. The permissive will of God comes quickly; it doesn't
tarry—speaking of the Devil.

Concerning Iifi, when I'm worshiping God in spirit and in
truth, would to God that I could convert that spiritual state into the
physical state. The feeling is ecstasy and the joy is endless and the
revelation is perfect. Once I'm back to the physical state it's difficult to
capture that spiritual state. It's all about staying optimistic in the flesh
and keeping the faith and believing that what the Spirit reveals will
manifest itself.

God saw the end from the beginning. But in Isaiah 48:7, God
asserts that He creates something new today which wasn't created in
the beginning. So if God creates something new today that wasn't
created in the beginning, it implies that for God, the end is more
important than the beginning; it implies that God's will for us could
change but we wouldn't know.

If it wasn't in God's will for Iifi to be my wife, I summon my
God saying, "God please have mercy upon me, I know my life has
already been written. Give Iifi to me as my wife. This is your world
there is nothing you can't do. Let my prayers be in Your will, Lord
God my Heavenly Father."

God saw the end from the beginning; God knew that this day
will come that I will seek Him for Iifi to be my wife. Nothing is news
to God; my prayers to God are not news to Him. God knew me before
I was born. I didn't just wake up one morning and start demanding

and requesting to the Lord that I yearned for Iifi to be my wife; the befalling of events led to my request.

Isaiah 48 verse 6 and 7 says, "I have shewed thee new things from this time, even hidden things, and thou didst not know them. They are created now and not from the beginning." So I prayed to God that He should suffer Iifi to be my wife now if she wasn't meant to be my wife from the beginning of time. God wouldn't let His words come back to Him void, so let Him create Iifi to be my wife now; give her hands to me in marriage.

I made a promise, even a covenant, to God that comes with a stipulation. I guaranteed my Lord God my Heavenly Father that I will never abandon Him for Iifi once He gives His daughter to me for a wife. And I requested for Lucifer to be a witness to my very prayer that I uttered to the Lord.

In the fall of 2012, as I was walking up and down and to and fro in a certain area of New Jersey, the spirit of Lucifer came by my side and told me (paraphrasing), "Nndy do you think that God is an ordinary God? How long are you going to fast and pray for Iifi to be your wife? If God is an awesome God and the God of Abraham, Isaac, and Jacob then let Him suffer Iifi to be your wife." So I took heed from the spirit of Lucifer and proceeded to beseech the Almighty God if He is an ordinary God or if He is the Almighty God in Heaven on high. "Are you the Lord God Almighty?"

I summoned my Lord that if Iifi is not my wife then I will consider Him as an "ordinary God," not the God of Jesus Christ and the God of the Holy Spirit but rather the God of the unbelievers. I later repented for my utterance to God.

I absolutely leave God with no room to escape in not granting Iifi as my wife. I took advantage of the invincible wisdom God has given me. Hence, I uttered before God prayers that can be possibly only conceived with utmost wisdom. And the Holy Spirit is my witness.

God declared the end from the beginning; God Almighty saw the end of time on earth from the beginning of time on earth. God formed me and Iifi before the foundation of the world. I prayed to God on numerous occasions to remember the day that He saw me and Iifi getting married.

God's will is for me and Iifi to be married, that is why He perfected my worship of Him, because by asking God to give Iifi as my wife I am worshiping Him in season and out of season, and that has made my worship of God perfect.

Love of Iifi

The love that I have for Iifi is pure love from God because God knows that if I had stumbled upon or heard anything immoral about Iifi that I would cease from loving her.

I'm a man with Victorian principles. God knows that I take no prisoners in any way, shape, or form.

I unequivocally choose Iifi over anything in this world. Iifi is God's virgin daughter. I love her to death. I will die for her. The love I have for Iifi is the utmost love of my life; she is the only mortal of who I'm in awe.

If I had been a fornicator or a womanizer then I would have bowed out of my request for Iifi to be my wife. I won't have any credibility to stand before God and pray desirously for Iifi as a wife.

God is aware of the utmost love I have for Iifi. On the other hand, God also knows that my love for Him is second to none. So if God doesn't suffer Iifi to be my wife then God is jealous of the love I have for Iifi. In interpretation, God Almighty isn't keen for the love I have for Him to be threatened.

So the only way God could curtail the love I have for Iifi is not to heed to my request, even my supplication. But by any stretch of the imagination my unconditional love for Iifi doesn't threaten my immeasurable love for God Almighty. Just has I have retained all the love I have for God Almighty, I have retained all the love I have for Iifi.

Regardless, there is no comparison between how much I love Iifi and how much I love my Lord and Savior, because God's is an eternal love; it lasts forever. Iifi's is earthly love; it's only but temporary. God is righteous, true, and holy. Iifi is a sinner just like I am. I can't love sin more than I love righteousness. If so, I will defile myself. I can't love earth more than I love the Word of God because Heaven and earth shall pass away but the Word of God remains forever. And Nndy and Iifi are part of the Word of God.

I have received criticisms that I worship Iifi. But how can I accept that Iifi is my idol when I pray without ceasing to God

Almighty for her to be my wife? There is nowhere in the Bible that the children of Israel prayed to God Almighty for the upkeeping of Baal their idol.

I beseeched God to set Iifi free to love me because I know how much Iifi loves me but certain ungodly spirits are hindering her. My request for Iifi to be a helpmeet is not a battle against Man; rather, it's a battle against Satan, even that old serpent. Hence, the last verse of John chapter 17 was the last major prayer I prayed to God Almighty to defeat the ungodly spirit countering Iifi's love for me.

As God and Jesus are one, so also are me and Iifi. We are but one. As Jesus loved Man even more than He loved Himself, I told God that is how much I loved Iifi. Can I forget to say "in Jesus' name" after I finish uttering a prayer? I can't ever forget Iifi in my prayers.

John 17:26 "And I have declared unto them thy name, and will declare it: that the love wherewith thou hast loved me may be in them, and I in them." The perfect love of God is the love that God had for His only begotten Son. It's the purest and truest of all love that has ever existed in Heaven and on earth. That love, that perfect love, was my last important prayer I uttered to God in regard to me and Iifi. I prayed for that perfect love to exist between Iifi and me. But how could such a perfect love warrant God sending His only Son to come and die for the whole of mankind? How could such love be tampered with and compromised in such great depth? As much as I love Iifi, I wouldn't dare even think of giving her to be killed or crucified, for crying out loud.

Iifi is my God-given inheritance, so it's not a matter of sowing in order to reap. I love Iifi without reservation. I love Iifi to death, even unto eternal life. Iifi is the whole nine yards of love in my life. Iifi is the apple of my eye. God could make Iifi to be my wife; God can use my love and make Iifi my wife.

It's easy to say you love somebody but it is not easy to prove that love that you profess.

God said He loves us; hence, He sent Jesus to die for us. He showed it. God knows to what extent I love Iifi. God knows that she is the only mortal, that without second thought, I will die for. And my unreserved love for Iifi perhaps threatens my love for God Almighty.

Iifi is God's reserved. God has kept Iifi clean as a wind-driven snow; hence, He suffered me not to hear any immoral perverted tidings about Iifi because He knew this day was coming that I would seek Iifi to be my wife. And all the time I tried in vain to reach her and she ignored me is because it wasn't time for God's will to be fulfilled. So all my effort wasn't in vain, but it was God's plan from the onset.

I assured the Almighty that I will never stop worshiping Him if He gives Iifi to me as my wife, "but Father, regardless, I will still always worship You." The Devil salivates to know what I mean by "regardless." Does it mean that I will stop worshiping God if He doesn't give Iifi to me? If so Satan will petition to God every day for Iifi not to be my wife. Satan will be the happiest spirit ever once I cease from worshiping God because he is utterly jealous of my total unwavering devotion in worshipping God Almighty.

Journey to London

Let your belief in God be in reality as well as in imaginary; leave no stone unturned. For instance, I believe that God can use a true prophet to raise the dead; even though I have not seen or experienced it before, I believe wholeheartedly that it could happen. So in reality I haven't seen it happen before, but in imaginary I have seen it happen because I believe that God can do anything. With Him all things are possible.

Is America so morally corrupt that I had to journey to London to seek a wife? When it comes to marrying, all my eggs are in one basket. I ignored the popular adage of not putting "all one's eggs in one basket." And all the eggs were Iifi's. The basket belongs to God. Hence it wouldn't break.

Apart from the worshipping of God, I had to put Iifi first and foremost. All other things and concerns were put on the backburner. I had to let the dead bury their dead. I was tired of hearing, "What happened to Nndy? When are we going to hear that he got married?" Hence, I went to search for my missing rib in London.

In the last seven months before I purposed to see Iifi in London, I stayed on an "Iifi and Iifi only route," and I didn't make any detours until the mission, the destination, was fully completed, spiritually and physically. During that period, I had no time for any man on earth; the dead had to bury their dead. I sought the face of God lock, stock, and barrel—day in and day out for seven straight months. Every other obligation was an enemy to me so they were all cut off before consideration.

At the last minute of the eleventh hour, God revealed to me in a vision that Iifi will be my wife. It was also the last scheduled day of worshiping God in church too, even the last day of the Jewish holiday.

I sought a sign from God to know when to travel to London to see Iifi and how I would see her. And God marvelously answered my prayers, and to boot God provided the fare for the journey. After the event, I was clever to realize that just as God showed Abraham's servant where to go to see Rebekah for a wife for Isaac, He did for me too. And even though I had known Iifi in the past, even in Nigeria, those days were innocent.

In the vision, the dayspring from on high visited me. On the ninth day of the tenth month of 2012, God showed me a vision, and through a song, "Master the Tempest Is Raging," He revealed to me that I and Iifi will be together.

I thought the Most High God only brought the increase after Apostle Paul had planted and Apollos had watered? Faith without works is dead. Hence, I had to visit the United Kingdom to see Iifi.

When I was questioned what I will do if I don't marry Iifi, I responded by saying that it's either Iifi or no one. I didn't want the Devil to use my word on that front against me before the Almighty God. And when I was pressed I reiterated that I don't care about any other woman save Iifi. I reiterated that the Devil is always going to and fro, hence I wasn't going to give him words to use against me before God, so I declined to answers questions pertaining to that front.

I bid God in prayer a few days before I departed to see Iifi, let me never doubt in my belief and faith in God on this mission. Before my flight to London, I bid God that the same precious Holy Spirit that He has given to abide with me should also be given unto Iifi too—because God is omnipresent and since me and Iifi are one. In that way, there will be an agreement and no argument between me and Iifi because we are abided with the same Holy Spirit even unto death.

Can the servant fast forever? Can the servant fast when the master is home? How long will I have to fast? Until and when Iifi becomes my wife? When God didn't reveal the vision to me, I fasted day in and day out. But once God gave me the revelation, my fasting was moderated. That is after God had told me in a vision and in a dream that Iifi will be my future wife.

I said boldly to my beloved godfather, Sir Ukonne that even if Iifi is a witch I will marry her. I said this because I would never give any room for an alternative. It's either Iifi or no one. He said, "God knows what is best for you and He has someone good for you." And in response I said that I don't yearn for someone that is deemed "good for me" because I'm not living this life on earth forever. So just give me Iifi because my stay on earth is only but temporary. He said Iifi will be a "young widow," and then elaborated that "God's thought and God's ways are not Man's. And He knows what is best for us." I know that already; its gospel to me but I'm not giving God an alternative in all my prayers that I'm requesting, except my prayers for Iifi. If I'm praying to God and giving Him no alternative in all my prayers to Him, then would I be demanding parity with the Lord? In replying, he maintained that "I don't know her that well." And in response I said, "I don't care to know her well before I marry her, I just want to marry her, period. The fact that God made me to love her in the beginning, was that a mistake? Why is asking the Almighty to give her to me now an issue? I thought God saw the end from the beginning? So why, all of a sudden, am I being accused of not giving God an alternative in my petition for Him to suffer me to marry Iifi? The fact that God suffered me to love Iifi means that I would start without finishing if I don't marry her. God has never started without finishing." How do you expect me to marry a woman who wasn't there from the beginning? Why can't I espouse Iifi whom I have loved on the first day? Why should I espouse someone else who I wouldn't know from Adam? I knew Iifi from Adam. Sir Ukonne said, "Let God solve my plight [betrothal] and take the bait." Because I have labored so long for Iifi; in parallel with Jacob's fourteen years to marry Rachel, I told God that I will never ask Him for a wife because I have already pled to Him time and time again that Iifi is who I want my wife to be. My Lord revealed her to me and God made me love Iifi, so my Lord has to pay the price for me to marry her. It's not a matter of my way or the highway, but for all the prayers and supplications uttered, it wouldn't be in vain. My Lord and Savior didn't create me in vain. This is no longer in the hands of Man; it's not even in the hands of Iifi; this is in the hands of God Almighty. This has reached a climax; a point of no return. Because if Iifi is not my wife, Satan will testify against my supplications before God; and God is a peaceful God. The last thing the Almighty God wants is to be constantly bombarded by Satan's rant.

The joy of marrying any woman save Iifi has past; the hangover is alive. Iifi is the lost sheep that I abandoned the ninety-nine for. The one that I supposed was my better half left without any reason, so why look for another? Wouldn't I suffer the same fate?

I got held up on my route to England; the spirits of London denied me entrance to London. I could imagine the spirits of London saying, "Why do you want to come and elope with one of our daughters back to America?" But at the last minute, God intervened and sweetened the heart of the London airport authorities; hence, I was let in after I was held up for exactly seven hours.

The stakes in life are too high; hence, there is no time to kill only one bird with one stone. But when I went to London to see Iifi, it was to kill one bird with one stone.

But because of wisdom, I had the shrewd ability to guiltily ascertain other birds that I killed innocently without intending to; albeit I sneezed at them.

My trip to London to see Iifi could be compared to Jesus coming to die for mankind. I have expressed to Iifi on a number of occasions via phone and mail that I love her so much, but all my words to her were like idle talk or fairytales. And Iifi seldom gave feedback—nothing substantial by any stretch of the imagination. And with all the messages I sent to her, she seldom dignified my messages with a response. I sent her a handful of messages. So instead of continuing doing what I did in the past, and continuing hiding behind technology, I had to take the leap of going to see her face to face. But Iifi was scared to see me because of how much love I have for her; she was scared to her bone because she couldn't fathom the unadulterated love that I have for her.

God Almighty expressed time and time again that He loved Man so much, but in order for God to prove that He truly, really loved Man, He had to come in a human form to die for Man whom He loved so much—and to boot, so that Man would be saved.

I was somewhat scared going to see Iifi because I didn't know the outcome of my visit and because of the dread of seeing the person that I love the most in this life. I was going to unchartered waters but if I didn't go, I would never have peace of mind. Jesus said don't let your heart be troubled. However, since I ventured to go, the ball is no longer in my court.

The scariest day of Iifi's life was when I went to see her. She was scared of the pure love I have for her. She was scared that reality had reared its head; it was no longer a fairytale; it was no longer something that happens in movies. Hence, she was perplexed, dumbfounded, and nonplussed; Iifi couldn't believe what had bechanced her.

Iifi took me as a celebrity and big shot when I came to London. It was the greatest feat in her life what she single handedly did.

I missed my non-refundable flight in London when I was returning to New York. The spirits of London were certain to give me their best shot; they made sure they severely dealt with me. But they forgot I was a New Yorker. My trip to London wasn't in vain because everything I do, the Holy Spirit in Person goes before me. He sent me to London and I followed the lead of the Holy Spirit. I don't go anywhere by my might or by my wisdom but by the leading of the Holy Spirit. I shook the dust off my feet in London and was homeward bound to New York City. It is not by might or by power but by God's spirit. The battle I'm fighting is not a physical battle; rather, it's a spiritual battle. I'm fighting against principalities and spirits, not against mortals. Criticism, incarceration, or prosecution can't make me change my attitude about Iifi because I'm fighting a spiritual battle for my wife, my helpmate, even as my missing rib. So I can't let what happens in the flesh take precedent.

The fulfillment of God's Word is Jesus Christ. God spoke the Word of God (Jesus) and the Word of God (Jesus) became flesh. My promise from God that Iifi will be my wife will be fulfilled just as

Christ was the fulfillment of the Word of God. I'm doing everything conceivable that I can do that will speed up God's promise for me regarding the Iifi front. I'm doing everything from chronicling everything that God has shown me, to tempting and deceiving myself in the fantasy of accommodating concubines—everything to speed up God's promise that it should no longer tarry.

Maybe I should keep my dreams to myself of marrying Iifi, instead of making them come true. But God has showed me great mercy in his revelations that Iifi will be wife. Iifi rejecting me is me rejecting women as a whole. But I pray it will not eventuate to that. It was the pure unadulterated love in me given by God Himself that made me do what I did regarding Iifi.

After Iifi abandoned and left me in the lurch, it was one of the lowest times of my life.

But "he that is down needs fear no fall." On the other hand, I'm still filled with joy because no Man in this earth has half of the wisdom that God has blessed me with. No Man in America, Europe, Africa, or on the seven continents is able to tie my shoe lace, wisdom-wise. You can take that to the bank. The day I condemn Iifi will never happen; Satan could fast all day and all night.

If it wasn't God that revealed to me that Iifi will be my wife, then God Himself would have to descend from Heaven to earth like He did to His prophets of old, before I can believe again. If a man of the cloth comes to me saying, "Thus saith the Lord . . .," I wouldn't believe except if the man were a total stranger. I will unequivocally doubt if it is really from God that spoke to me through a vision or through His vessels. It's only God Himself that has to visit me one on one before I can believe any message regarding Iifi. Because I will be lying to myself if I admit that I have faith if someone brings me a message about Iifi. The last thing I want is to live a life of doubt. So the ball is in my Heavenly Father's court.

Perfect Dream

In Heaven during the rebellion, Satan the Devil only took one third of the angels down with him when he didn't get what he desired from God Almighty. One third is insignificant to me; I won't accept one third if I don't get what I want from God Almighty in terms of Iifi. Iifi is worth more than one third.

I appealed before God that He should judge the stubbornness in my love for not giving up on Iifi and finally bless me with Iifi as the wife of my bosom. I entreat God to bless me for my stubbornness in not suffering Iifi to go.

God has dealt with me profoundly differently since when I wholeheartedly devoted my life to Him. I'm the epitome of the smallest minority; God has never dealt specifically with me the way He dealt with Man. So if my faith in God that Iifi will be my wife doesn't materialize then there will be more questions than answers. That day will never be conceived—that is how much faith I have in God. If God fashioned me to be unique all the time I have lived this life that He has given me on earth, then He wouldn't make me equal to the rest of mankind and suffer my reality to be the reality of Man.

If God the Father (not God the Son) in 1 Timothy chapter 3 could come down in the flesh just to preach to the Gentiles, then with God all things are possible. With God all things are possible. God made a way in the wilderness; God also made rivers in the desert. Hence, if God can turn the ocean into dry land on two occasions, asking God for Iifi to be my wife should be easy as pie for Him to do. If God can send His only begotten Son through an immaculate conception, asking God for Iifi to be my wife should be the icing on the cake. If God the Father could come down and preach to the Gentiles, then asking God for Iifi to be my wife should be for good measure before God; it should be the angel on the Christmas tree.

There is nothing absolutely that God can't do.

It is possible for Iifi to be my wife, for with God nothing is impossible.

Approximately two months after I returned from England, God revealed to me a perfect dream about Iifi. The dream I had about Iifi was as clear as day, so that I don't need a Joseph or a Daniel to interpret the dream for me. I watch my dreams closely. And as Joseph's dream came through, so my dream will come true. How can you love a dream more than you love reality? The dream was the "said" part of my last important prayer to God which is in John 17:26. And the "done" part will manifest when it eventually culminates in marrying Iifi.

Although my love for God is immeasurable, I told my Lord that I love Iifi so much that my love for Him is not completed without Iifi and I being together because my worship of God will be compromised. I have something of chief concern that disturbs me, which is Iifi and I not being together—unless I want to lie to myself. Would God I could lie to myself. But I can't.

At the beginning, God declared spiritually that He will create Man, and in the physical it manifested when Adam was created. All was "said," when God the Father, the Son, and the Holy Spirit said, "Let us create Man in our own image." And all was "done," when Adam was created from the dust of earth. God through His holy prophets "said" He will send His only begotten Son to come and die for us. And God's word manifested and was "done" when Christ came through the Immaculate Conception via the Virgin Mary. I'm three years older than my missing rib, so obviously the love God had for me was first manifested in the physical before the love God had for Iifi was manifested.

As I tarried for God's promise to manifest, it is what happens in the meantime that really matters. Lingering doubts of if Iifi is really worth it? Am I really in awe of Iifi? Is she really of the high esteem that I hold her to be? Or is she just an ordinary woman and not the beautiful angel that I perceive her to be?

I'm doing everything to complete my mission on earth. So I'm doing everything to marry Iifi; to let God's promise come to pass. I'm putting God in remembrance. While it tarried, while waiting for the fulfillment of God's promise, I would never sincerely and honestly seek the hands of any women. If I went against my word, there might be repercussions. I will continue to strive with God Almighty through unrelenting prayers until my Holy Grail of Iifi becoming my wife is manifested.

I take no pleasure in the things of this world. Iifi is all I want. I perceive that my worship for God will be at a permanent pinnacle once we get married. I need a challenge, and Iifi is the only mortal who could give me a challenge in this life on earth. She is my only weakness in this life. The end of Man's wisdom is upon me; I would have to be pretending that life is fine with me if my life is lived without Iifi. I would live a sorry life if my Lord doesn't grant Iifi as my wife because she is the only joy that I would have physically.

Nothing in life is a challenge to me save the things of God. Iifi is a challenge in life to me because it involves my ultimate and unshakable faith in God Almighty. After Iifi rejected me, I loved Iifi even more than before. I love what is difficult to get; I love what will give me a challenge; hence, Iifi.

God is a forerunner to my birth; God is a forerunner to Iifi my missing rib's birth. God is a forerunner to our proposed marriage and God is a forerunner to our death. Death is not good for Iifi but the Word of God is a respecter of no man. And Christ also once died.

After Adam blamed Eve for his downfall in Genesis 3:12, "And the Man [Adam] said, the woman whom thou gavest to be with me, she gave me of the tree, and I did eat"—Proverbs 18:22 justified the woman by saying, "Whoso findeth a wife findeth a good thing, and obtained favour of the Lord." The road to betrothing Iifi is hell; hence the outcome will be heaven. Marrying Iifi will be a heaven to me. My ultimate earthly goal, my holy grail on earth is to marry Iifi, while my ultimate spiritual goal is for me and Iifi to be in Heaven with my Lord and Savior.

Jesus intercedes for Iifi every day of her life, while I intercede for her on earth.

Iifi is my flesh and blood; I pay tithes at church on my behalf and on my missing rib's behalf. The paying of tithes is an important obligation for Christians. I take Holy Communion on our behalf too. Christ said believers should take Holy Communion because it represents His body and His blood. Iifi is my flesh and my blood. I have to leave no stone unturned.

In closing, I didn't push back at my unceremonious departure from London; I let the door hit me on my way out because I knew that I was commissioned by God. If you suffer God to always go before you, then everything that happens to you is God's will.

Spiritually, the Word of God keeps me honest, but I need my missing rib to keep me honest physically.

In terms of marrying Iifi, I will hold my breath. That is the measure of my extreme faith in God.

The day I condemn Iifi will be the day that I will realize how much Iifi loves me, so I will rather tarry for God's promise to be fulfilled. If I should condemn Iifi then it would be pretentious.

What is the number of breaths that Christ breathed while He was on earth? I tell you that every breath that Christ breathed on earth is in me and Iifi. In essence, our last breath belongs to Jesus.

The Scriptures was fulfilled after Jesus came and died for Man. In the meantime I'm waiting for the Scriptures of my life to be fulfilled; and that Scriptures to be fulfilled is betrothing Iifi. If God remembers the day Iifi and I will pass away, and if God remembers the day Iifi and I regenerate in Heaven with Him, then let Him, I pray, remember the day that He saw me and Iifi getting married.

Faith without work is dead, so I had to make the journey to London, thereby leaving the ball in God's court. God Almighty said "Let there be light" and there was light. God spoke faith out of Himself and faith manifested itself. So, too, do I speak faith to myself and beseech God, "Let Iifi be my wife." But Christ is the author and finisher of my faith.

"Father just as You remembered how Christ came and died for the sins of Man, God my Heavenly Father, I beseech You to remember when you saw me and Iifi getting married in Your presence, just as You remembered when You created the world in six days."

John 15 verse 7 says, "If ye abide in me and my word abides in you, ye shall ask what ye will and it shall be done unto you." Even if Iifi wasn't meant to be my wife, "Father, please, I know my life has already been written. This is Your world and there is nothing absolutely that my Lord can't do."

My worshipping of God was only made perfect by my endless singing and prayers to God for Iifi to be my wife. Having said that, my worship of God is perfect but it's not complete because at the end of the day, after worshiping God wouldn't the bitter taste of not yet betrothing Iifi come to my mouth? After worshiping God with my whole heart wouldn't I be back to reality with a sad countenance?

How high does Iifi want me to jump? There is no other option when it comes to marriage; it's either Iifi or the highway. It's safe to say that Iifi is my be-all and end-all, the end of the world, my celebrity, the whole nine yards of what is good to me—by and large, everything but my Savior.

Iifi is my hidden treasure. Proverbs 31:10-31 exemplifies the hallmark of a virtuous and a perfect wife, even the distinguished hallmarks of Iifi. I love Iifi unto eternal life; and being that I'm still living on earth, that means I love her more than I love myself because I love eternal life more than I love earthly, temporary life.

I have gone too deep in my daily supplications to God for Iifi to be my wife, that there is no way possible that Iifi can't be my wife. It's like if a man kills someone, the corpse is the evidence that someone was killed.

It speaks volumes that Iifi has never hauled insults at me. I love Iifi so much because I have never lived a prostituting and promiscuous lifestyle. I lived an abstained lifestyle, yet I'm still the most sinful person in this world. The only love that surpasses the love I have for Iifi is the love I have for the Potter, even the Almighty God on high.

I told God that Him and Him alone can cause me and my missing rib to get married. Only He can grant me my heart's desire. God could easily make me to stop loving Iifi. He could put me in a vegetative state and send me into a coma, thereby making me to forget Iifi.

The beginning of my love for women is Iifi; hence, the end of my love for women has to be Iifi. Christ killed so many birds with one stone when He died for me and Iifi to be saved, and one of the birds He killed was for me and Iifi to be married.

I left no stone unturned in my prayers to God. As I beseeched the precious Holy Spirit that as He came upon the Virgin Mary to conceive Jesus my Lord, so too the Holy Spirit should be upon Iifi, so that she would conceive marital love for me.

God already knows our desires. Let God's will be done.

All my loved ones, are they not mentioned in our first autobiography?

LET THE MIND THAT WAS IN CHRIST JESUS BE IN YOU ALL. AMEN

Thanks

Live forever, Ifiok Ekwere, O daughter of the Highest; God bless her family and kindred. Live forever, Ntiense Malik Nenty, thou son of the Lamb; God bless his family and kindred. Live forever, Imo Ukonne, daughter of the Almighty; God bless her family and kindred. Nancy Samson-Etim, Miles and the Samson-Etim family. Henty, Felecia, Nse, Harry, Andrew, Nsongura, Mfon and the Nenty's family as a whole. Charles, Emmanuel, Godwin and the Ebbi family; Margaret Mendie and the entire Mendie family, Edidiong, Udema, Aniekan, Uyime and the Nenty family; Ebebe and the Ebebe family.

God bless Bassey, Florence, and the Ekpenyoug family; God bless Linda Uko, thou faithful daughter of the Most High, Charles, James, and the Uko family; God bless Samuel, Arit, Ini, and the Ukonne family; God bless the household of Kutama and Emen Nenty; God bless the household of Eyakeno, Inietop, Nsitie, Stella and the Obot family. Eteino, Ofonbuk, Nsifiok and the Etuk family; Emen, Oto-Obong, Imo and the Idio Ebu and Alice Ebu family; Eddy, Mboboswo and the Blessing Utin family; Vanessa and Princes Inietop Udom and family; Uche and family; Celestine Ntwen and family; Akpan Ebere and family; Okoro Etukudo and family, God blessing is upon all your household. Veronica and Unwana Nenty-God bless thou daughters of Heaven; Edima Isua, thou faithful daughter of the Holy One, Idong Isua and the whole Isua and Ntem family; Ubong, Ndifreke and the Ntawo family; Celestine Mohammed and the Mohammed family; Charles, Margaret, George and the Archibong family; Henrietta, o special daughter of God the Father; Tolu, Bolu and the Kupoluyi family; Benji Igbine and the Igbine family; Sharafa and the Salaudeen family; Adikan and the Ekpanya family; Anita, Nina Momodu Johnson and the Momodu family; Oliyide Afolabi Sobiye and the Sobiye family; Obinna Odumodu and the Odumodu family; Daniel, David, Nancy Ogulu and the Ogulu family; Mark Hoskins and the Hoskins family; Esther Uko, Michael Uko, Ashley, Marie, Nina, Devin, Rebel, Basquin and the Ancient of Days family, God bless you all. Rick Santorum and family; Ini Orok and the Orok family; Kufre Uwah, Chidi, Kelechi Uka and the Uka family, Emem Udoimok and the Udoimuk family, Kufre, Ndifreke, Edidiong, Unyime and the John family; Chima Ikonne and family; Ofonime and the Essien family; Nicolas Utsao, Odiong Akpan, John Osim, Ifiok Robinson, Mfon Peters, Etim-Oyo Ita, Aniekan Ekwere and Okorn

Frank and the Unical, Calabar family; Mark Excel, Anna and family; Israel Steinberg; Jay, Bunzo Osusely, Eyen, Enos, Eutah, Moris, Shem, Sean, Peter, Matthew, Egor, Denise, Amir, Julian, Gershwin, Bryon, Mark, Thomas, Mohammedu, Lyno and the MBS/Tri State family; John, Akaninyene, Charity and Isidor Ebebe; Nnamdi, Obinna, Ijeoma, Chinazo and the Ihim family; Zelise Mazyck and family, God bless you all. Odon, Joel, Ubengama, Margaret Ukonne, Akaninyene Jacob, Bertha and the Ikot Ama family; Nsima Nenty, and the Qua-Ibo family; Thomas, Prince, Samuel, Imo, Alice, Mfon and the Ukeh family; Tom DeLay and family; Unyime Celestine Akpan and family; Angela, Bridget, Keith, Mark, Supreme, Indy and the Brooklyn family; Stefeni, Chris and the Long Island family; Eyen Ibibio, Mfon, Aniekan, Carni, Uyo Ukonne and the New Jersey family; Niyi, Theo, Ib, Daniel, Ndifreke Ukoette and the Lagos family; Sarah Palin, Mark Levin and the conservative family; Junior Akpan and the Lesotho family; William Etukudo; Cecilia and Akpan family; Rose Kimelman and family; Bernadine, Nathaly, Adriana, Charles, Leeyana, Nina Arroyo, and the LIU family. Kuzo, Kozo, Kalu; Kelechi, Sunday, Silva and the Toyibat family; Ebong, Kazeem, Toshitit and the London family; Victor Udensi, Mercy Ekeng, Nelly, Adam, Cecelida, Zane Searchwell and the New York family, God bless you all children of the Holy Father. God bless Stanley and Steven Howse, Bryon McCane, Anthony Henderson, Charles Scruggs and the Cleveland, Ohio family. God bless Sean and Jill Hannity and family; Steven Gerrard, Daniel Agger, Lucas Leiva; Luis Suarez, Jose Reina, Glen Johnson, Jamie Carragher, Martin Skrtel—God bless; Fernando Torres, Jose Enrique, Philip Coutinho, Xabi Alonso, Javier Marcherano, Daniel Sturridge, Brendan Rodgers, Rafa Benitez, Kenny Dalglish, Victor Moses, Henderson, Suso, and Sterling—God bless Liverpool FC; God bless Rush and Kathryn Limbaugh and family; finally God bless Ndinanake Ukeh O thou marvelous daughter of the Almighty, live forever.

FOOTNOTE

Rush Limbaugh; the Media on Obama and Me—The Rush Limbaugh Show www.rushlimbaugh.com › Archives (Aug 26, 2013);

Rush Limbaugh; Rush on Fox News Channel's the Five—The Rush Limbaugh Show www.rushlimbaugh.com › Archives (Jul 10, 2013);

Rush Limbaugh; Why People Think Democrats Care—The Rush Limbaugh Show www.rushlimbaugh.com › Archives (Jun 21, 2013).